CW00485419

Manchester United®
PRIDE
OF ALL EUROPE

THE OFFICIAL ROAD TO GLORY IN THE 1998/99 CHAMPIONS' LEAGUE

BY ALEX LEITH FOREWORD BY ALEX FERGUSON

**First published in 1999 by
Manchester United Books
An imprint of André Deutsch Ltd
76 Dean Street
London W1V 5HA
www.vci.co.uk**

Text copyright © Manchester United
Books 1999

The right of Alex Leith to be identified as the
author of this work has been asserted by him in
accordance with the Copyright, Designs and
Patents Act 1988.

All rights reserved. This book is sold subject to
the condition that it may not be reproduced,
stored in a retrieval system or transmitted in any
form or by any means, electronic, mechanical,
photocopying, recording or otherwise without
the Publisher's prior consent

A catalogue record for this book is available
from the British Library

ISBN 0 233 99771 7

Printed in Italy

10 9 8 7 6 5 4 3 2 1

A Zone production

Design: David Hicks, Andy Smith
Copy editor: Stephanie Jones
Picture editor: Matt Turner

Cover photograph: Action Images
Photographs: Action Images, Allsport,
Hulton Getty, Empics, Colorsport
Statistics supplied by Carling Opta

Special thanks to:
Alex Ferguson, Jim Drewett,
Lou Pepper, Faith Mowbray,
Di Law, Rebecca Tow, Rose Allison,
Paul Steggle, Richard Deal

Contents

I'm so proud of my players

by Alex Ferguson

When you go in for a competition, whatever competition, then you want to win the trophy at the end of it. I'd never set the European Cup as the one trophy I wanted to win, it wasn't until I joined United, in fact, that I thought I had a genuine chance of winning it. I went in for the competition three times with Aberdeen, we had a young team and although they got to the quarter-finals once I never really thought I had a chance of winning it with them. But with United, especially in the last two or three years, I've felt we've been getting closer all the time and now we've done it, we've won the Champions' League and I'm very, very proud.

The team that won in 1968 deserved all the accolades, they still do, and now this team deserves all their accolades. On a personal level, it has been nice to relive the glory of 1968. People often ask me about Matt Busby or myself and being the most successful Manchester United manager ever. But that's not something that drives me at all. I think for me, the drive comes from achievement, from us now having won the European Cup and that is enough for me. It has been a great achievement for all of us.

Throughout the campaign, the only time I felt a bit vulnerable was the first Barcelona game, in the group stage, at Old Trafford. We were 2–0 up at half time and yet we only just escaped with a 3–3 draw in the end because Barcelona played very well in the second half and we had a man sent off. But there was a period during that match when I thought, we've still got a bit to go yet before we can match the likes of Barcelona. But by the time we got to the Nou Camp for the return leg, they needed a win to go through to the quarter-finals. We played very well and so did they, but we put them out and it was then I realised that maybe yes, we were ready for it.

The new players we brought in this season

have definitely helped. Blomqvist, Yorke and Stam have been excellent and they've given us the sort of back-up you need. I thought last year in the quarter-final against Monaco that we had a good team, but you can't win the European Cup without a good squad. I think this year the difference was that we've had the back-up of a pool of players who are capable of playing at the highest level.

There's always a learning curve for players, especially the young ones and we've got lots of youngsters in the team: the Nevilles, the Butts the Beckhams who are in their early twenties still so it's always going to be a learning process for them, but they've taken great strides this year. It's important for the team spirit and the success of the club that we've been able to produce players who have grown up within the club and developed an understanding for it. That has had, and will continue to have, a big big part to play in our success.

And we have to build on our success and improve. There are always ways to improve yourselves, and now that we've won this trophy, we have to find ways to go forward. If we keep improving, then maybe we can become like Liverpool who were the dominant side of the 1970s and 1980s.

Next season the competition will be bigger again, with more games. We'll need an even stronger pool because if we want to get to the final, we will have had to play a total of 17 matches, and with internationals and the domestic programme then we're going to need a bigger squad of players, which will enable us to make challenges in all the competitions we enter. And we will be challenging and hoping to emulate the success we've had this season, because yes, we're champions of Europe, but there is always room to improve and that's what we'll be aiming to do.

Alex Ferguson

Campioni

European champions United celebrate their miraculous win

Fergie lifts his Holy Grail

Nev, Becks and Stam in wonderland

Medallion men Yorke and Cole celebrate

Becks puts his foot in it

Johnsen gets in between the goalscorers

Pete takes a tumble

The grin red line

Agony and ecstasy

Olé, Olé

Now you're Gunnar believe us

The competition's top scorer lifts the trophy

Three-minute hero Solskjaer

Scholes and Keane, cruelly excluded from playing, join in the celebrations

He went to Man United and he won it all

Neville Neville land

10 CAMPIONI

The great Dane

Manchester knighted

The cup's in safe hands

Boot boy Giggs salutes the fans

What a way to finish

Smells like team spirit

Glory glory Man United

Great Scot

CHAPTER **2** 2.1

The boys of '68

How United won the European Cup at Wembley

The Boys of '68

EUROPEAN CUP FINAL	29 May 1968	Wembley Stadium	Att: 100,000	Entertainment: 100%

Manchester United 4 Benfica 1 United: Charlton, 2, Best, Kidd Benfica: Garcia

At the beginning of the 1967/1968 season, Matt Busby had been managing Manchester United for a highly eventful 22 years. In that time the Scotsman had nurtured three great teams and won four League championships and two FA Cups. He was the most successful United manager in the history of the club, but he had never won the biggest competition in domestic football, the European Cup, and, like Alex Ferguson 30 years later, the trophy had become his Holy Grail. Particularly as his greatest team of all, the Busby Babes, had been decimated during the Munich air disaster when eight players had died on their way back from a successful quarter-final in Belgrade. As Munich survivor Bobby Charlton later said, "If the crash had happened during an FA Cup run we would have chased after that. But it took place during the European Cup and things wouldn't have been right till we'd won that."

The closest United had come was in 1966, when they won through to the semi-finals after a superb victory over the Juventus of the day, Benfica. The Portuguese champions had participated in four of the five previous finals, winning twice. At Old Trafford, United had won an exhilarating first leg against the Eusebio-inspired side 3–2, which wasn't thought to be enough to get through the tie. Busby had urged his men to defend that lead in Lisbon (eschewing their normal attacking policy) but they had ignored him and sensationally won 5–1, with three goals in the first 15 minutes. Best scored two and performed so well he was nicknamed 'O Beatle' and was chased around the ground afterwards by adoring Portuguese fans. Even Benfica's score was a stunning volleyed own goal by full back Shay Brennan. However United had gone down 2–0 in the first leg of the semi against an uncompromising Partisan Belgrade side (with Denis Law missing

a crucial open goal) and had only won 1–0 at Old Trafford with Best out injured and Paddy Crerand sent off. Nobby Stiles' scurried goal was not enough. It must have seemed like the end of the world to Busby.

But you never give up the quest for the Holy Grail. Busby pressed on, and in May 1967 United reached the European Cup again by winning the League championship on the last day of season's play with a superb 6–1 victory at Upton Park against the great West Ham of Moore, Hurst and Peters. Within a week, Celtic had become the first British side to lift the European Cup, and Busby tried to sign their winger Jimmy Johnstone, as well as World Cup hero Geoff Hurst from West Ham. Neither deal was finalised, though Busby was happy with the development of a number of youngsters, especially 18-year-old Brian Kidd, who had starred in a pre-season tour of the States and Australasia. A first-round European Cup draw against Hibernian seemed tough – until it turned out to be Hibernian of Malta rather than Scotland. United beat the part-timers 4–0 at Old Trafford (two goals apiece from Bobby Charlton and David Sadler) and drew 0–0 on a bumpy Mediterranean pitch.

Next up were European novices FK Sarajevo, the Yugoslav team who had scraped through

Foot soldiers

When Matt Busby first became United's manager, in February 1945, he was still a sergeant-major in the army. He served in the war as manager of the army team whose job it was to entertain troops just behind the Italian front. Players in the team included Tommy Lawton, Joe Mercer and Frank Swift.

Get in there! Denis Law scores in the famous 5–1 win over Benfica in 1966

The beginning of the road to glory. United get ready to parade the League trophy in 1967

What a season...
Manchester City won the League championship, pipping United to the post by winning 4–3 at St James' Park on the last day of the season. United lost 2–1 at home to Sunderland.
Alan Mullery became the first England player to be sent off when dismissed in the European Championship semi-final in June. England lost the match 1–0, but finished third (their highest ever placing) after beating the Soviet Union in the play-off. Jimmy Hill (above) quit as Coventry manager having taken them from the Third Division to the first and completely overhauled and modernised the club. He became a TV pundit.
The English transfer record was twice broken in the season, with Tottenham buying Martin Chivers from Southampton for £125,000, and Leicester paying Fulham £150,000 for Allan Clarke.
In the season opener, the Charity Shield, United keeper Alex Stepney conceded a goal to his opposite number Pat Jennings who had cleared from his own area. The match finished 3–3.
West Bromwich Albion beat hot favourites Everton to lift the FA Cup with a rare left-foot goal from Jeff Astle.
Leeds broke their trophy duck by winning the League Cup against Arsenal, then went one better by beating Ferencváros of Hungary in the Fairs Cup Final.

the previous round against Cyprus' Nicosia. In front of 35,000 passionate fans, United found the going tough in Yugoslavia and Musemic of Sarajevo had what seemed a valid goal disallowed when Stepney clawed his shot back from over the line. 0–0. At Old Trafford, United were lucky to go through. They went in front when the Sarajevo keeper could only parry a Best header, and Aston netted the rebound. Prljaca was then sent off for a retaliatory foul on Best, who scored a second, but only after the ball had seemingly gone over the line. Then Sarajevo scored a comeback goal through Delalic. United held on, but were not convincing winners, with Sarajevo's team still bemoaning the ref's dodgy decision in the first leg, which would have put them through on the new away-goals rule.

In the next round, Polish champions and seasoned European Cup campaigners, Gornik Zabrze, came to Old Trafford on the back of a decisive victory over crack Soviet side Dynamo Kiev. United, without the injured Denis Law, piled forward but it took them an hour to put the ball past the agile keeper Kostka. Or, to be

more exact, to watch the luckless Florenski put the ball in his own net. Kidd scored another late on to give United a total to defend against in Katowice. And defend they did, two weeks later, on a snow-covered pitch in deepest Silesia. It was so cold that many of the 105,000 strong crowd lit bonfires on the terraces. The first half was played in a dense blizzard; when the weather calmed down in the second, Zabrze's Lubanski scored a goal to tatter United's nerves. But their defence held out and once again, for the third time in their history, United had reached the semi-finals.

That Juventus were the easiest option in the semi-final draw was testament to the strength of the competition. But United drew the Spanish champions Real Madrid, winners of the competition in 1966, who had been in eight of the preceding 12 finals and won the first five competitions on the trot. Long gone were the likes of Puskas and Di Stefano: but Gento was still around and Pirri and Sanchis were almost worthy successors. Again United

continued on page 22

SIR MATT'S WEMBLEY

Pat Crerand Brought up in the Gorbals district of Glasgow, the (almost) complete midfielder was bought into United from Celtic in 1962 for the then-princely sum of £55,000. He was streetwise off the pitch and had great vision on it – he was an imaginative long-passer with grit in his tackle. His only drawbacks were a lack of pace and a hot temper that often got him in trouble. He was a great favourite with Matt Busby who treated him like a son, but once the great man left the club, Crerand's days were numbered. Crerand played 392 games for United, scoring 19 times.

George Best A few days after the young Best, a slip of a lad, had arrived at Old Trafford he slipped away and took a boat back to Belfast. He was soon back, with an imprint of his father's boot on his backside, and he went on to play his way into Old Trafford legend. Best was nominally a winger, who could beat the best of defenders with a slip of his hips and a lightning fast dribble. But as well as making goals for the likes of Law, Best could score them, too, his best season coming in the 1967/68 European Cup-winning season when he bagged a total of 28 in the League alone. Best spent 11 years at the club, scoring a total of 178 goals in 466 games before going off the rails at his peak.

Jimmy Murphy, The team's assistant manager first impressed Matt Busby when they met in the army. Although Busby was the triumphant 1968 team's inspiration and guiding light, Murphy – a former West Brom and Wales inside half – was undoubtedly its unsung hero. "Without Jimmy a lot of us would never have made it as footballers," said Wilf McGuinness. "At times we almost hated him because he drove us so hard. But it was always for our own good and we certainly respected him." Murphy even turned down offers to manage Brazil and Juventus to stay with United.

Brian Kidd The younger generation of United fans know Kiddo for the punishing training routines he put the first team through as Fergie's assistant before going off to manage Blackburn at the end of 1998. Older fans could never forget his performances up front for the Reds, especially his astonishing performance in the 1968 Final when, in the team to replace the injured Denis Law and bang on his 19th birthday, he scored United's third and clinching goal. It was one of 70 he scored in 264 appearances for the club before he moved away from his home town to Arsenal for £110,000 in 1974.

Sir Matt Busby is a name that will live forever in football folklore. Born just outside Glasgow, he played for Manchester City but when war broke out he joined the army. When he came out he was offered the job as manager of Manchester United. The rest, as they say, is history He served United for 25 years, building two great teams always centred around players who had come through the youth system. One great team – the 'Busby Babes' – was destroyed by the tragedy at Munich, the one he built to replace them won the European Cup. Sir Matt died in January 1994, but the legend lives on.

Alex Stepney Matt Busby paid Chelsea £60,000 for Stepney in the close season of 1966. London-born Stepney had only played one game for the Blues, having been bought from Millwall, because of the form of incumbent keeper Peter Bonetti. His job was to fit into the gloves of the great Harry Gregg, a tough task that had proved beyond trainees Gaskell and Dunne. Stepney, of course, went on to become an Old Trafford legend, playing 532 games for the club over 12 years, and keeping a record 170 clean sheets (only broken by Peter Schmeichel in 1999). 'Big Al', as he was nicknamed by his team-mates, even scored a couple of penalties into the bargain.

Bobby Charlton On 6 October 1956 just short of his 19th birthday, Bobby Charlton made his first of an incredible 754 appearances for the club after shining for two years in the youth and reserve teams. It was a debut which saw him score two goals, despite carrying an injured ankle that he hadn't admitted to Matt Busby. In his 17 years at Old trafford, Bobby became a world legend, his name being the only two words of English many foreigners ever got to know. Originally used as a winger (which he hated) Bobby soon became a deep-lying centre-forward with a legendary thumping shot that accounted for many of his 247 goals for the club. Sir Bobby remains England's top scorer with 49 goals in 106 games for the national side.

WONDERS FROM 1968

John Aston The son of his namesake father, a full back (and sometimes forward) Aston was a United legend in the '40s and '50s and later the Reds' youth-team coach. A left winger, he was pacy and direct, but noticeably less skilful and imaginative than the other forwards in the great United side of the late '60s. Nevertheless, he was an important member of the 1968 European Cup-winning team, chipping in with one of the quarter-final goals that helped put out Gornik Zabrze. In all, he netted 27 goals in 185 appearances for the Reds in his eight-year spell at the club.

Bill Foulkes The ultimate stopper: good in the air; safe on the ground with a body that was joked to be quarried from granite. Foulkes was one of the survivors of the Munich disaster. He made his debut in 1954 (after a short career as a miner in the St Helens pits, and played until he was 37. Ironically nicknamed 'PB' or Popular Bill for his taciturn nature, he captained the side after Munich and went on to make 689 appearances for the club, scoring 9 goals, including the vital equaliser in the 1968 European Cup semi-final against Real Madrid.

David Sadler In his ten-year spell at Old Trafford, Sadler was a model professional. Modest, elegant and well-behaved, he was Busby's dream, and, costing just £750 from Maidstone, was a snip. An elegant defender who could also play in midfield, or even up front, he lived in digs with George Best as a youngster and shared hotel rooms with him throughout his Man United career. Of the 27 goals he scored in his 333 games for the club, the most important was the crucial second in United's 3–3 semi-final draw with Real Madrid at the Bernebeu.

Tony Dunne Signed from Shelbourne in Ireland for £6,000 as a boy reserve after being discovered by Billy Behan, he commanded a regular full- back position, on either side of the field, at the club for 13 years. A Dubliner with a clever sense of humour, Dunne was a neat, tidy defender, good at tackling and unwilling to give the ball away: a prototype Denis Irwin. He played 530 games for United, scoring two goals, in the period between 1960 and 1973.

Shay Brennan A product of Matt Busby's youth team policy, Shay Brennan was a footballing full back ironically nicknamed 'the Bomber' for his classy style of play. Drafted into the team immediately after the Munich air disaster (he scored two debut goals from the wing) Shay became one of the most popular players at the club: a night owl, a mickey-taker with a broad local accent. His Irish parentage gave him the chance to play for the Republic, which he did 19 times. In total, he was at the club 13 years, scoring six goals.

Denis Law Signed from Italian giants Torino in the summer of 1962 for £115,000 (Torino had brought him from Huddersfield), he went on to become a United legend. It was testament to the strength of the '68 side that they won the European Cup without him. In total, Law scored 171 goals in 305 league appearances in a United shirt but in cup competitions his figures were even more impressive. The deadly Scotsman netted 28 goals in 33 matches in Europe and 34 goals in 44 appearances in the FA Cup. Nicknamed 'The Demon King', Law was voted European Footballer of the Year in 1964. As well as missing United's most glorious moment through injury, he suffered from knee trouble again in the early '70s and in July 1973 he was given a free transfer in recognition of his services. He moved to Manchester City, and in 1974 his back-heeled goal at Old Trafford effectively relegated United and was one of the least celebrated goals of all time.

Nobby Stiles A tough-tackling local lad who, from the age of six, used to go to Old Trafford with his dad before he made his club debut in 1960. Norbert has gone down in history as a destroyer, but in truth he was a talented midfielder, a brilliant man-marker and a myopic who occasionally badly mistimed his tackles. Nicknamed 'Happy', Stiles could intimidate the best of them, but what is often forgotten is his great reading of the game, his ability to intercept passes, and his unflagging stamina. A defender for the 1968 Final, Stiles was predominantly a holding midfielder, a role he fulfilled with excellence in the 1966 World Cup-winning team. In all, he played 392 games for United, scoring 19 goals.

were drawn at Old Trafford first; again they won through, though a single Best goal didn't give them much leeway on a warm May night in the famous Bernebeu stadium.

Thousands of United fans made the trip to Madrid to witness one of the great matches in United's history. Just days earlier, most of them had witnessed their team lose 2–1 to Sunderland at Old Trafford and hand the League championship to rivals Manchester City. They knew this was their only chance of glory that season, and the only way to qualify for the next European Cup was to win the competition outright. Busby decided to use the 5–3–2 defensive tactics that had allowed his team to scrape through in Poland, but at half time, he was forced to change tack. Real took the game to the English from the start and forced a lead on 30 minutes with a header by Pirri. Gento soon made it 2–0, and although an own goal pulled one back for United, Amancio scored a third before half time. It was a demoralised United who returned to the dressing room – 3–1 on the night, 3–2 on aggregate.

At half time Busby, who must have felt as low as his players, reminded them that the away-goals rule meant they only needed one goal to qualify. He also moved Sadler up front to join Kidd and Best (this was in the days before substitutes) and United retook the initiative in the second period. Bill Foulkes was the unlikely assist to Sadler who stole between defenders and goalkeeper to pull

one back. And it was the stopper, unused to being in the opposing half in open play, who sealed the tie for United in the 75th minute. He ignored anguished calls from the dug-out to make an unaccustomed run into the box, received the ball from George Best, and slotted it past the keeper. United, for the first time in their history, were in the Final.

Wembley had been chosen at the start of the season as the venue for the one-leg Final. Benfica, who had beaten Juventus home and away in the semis and who still featured the great Eusebio, were the opponents. United took the field in blue so as not to clash with Benfica's red and white. The whole country, still celebrating England's Wembley win in 1966, was captivated by the event – it was the first time an English club had reached such heights at club level. Children who could produce a valid ticket for the game were excused the day off school; millions tuned in at home on their black and white (and occasionally colour) TV sets. United's team news was not good: Denis Law, whose knee had been giving him

Semi-retirement
United reached the semi-final of the European Cup again the next season only to lose out 2–1 on aggregate to AC Milan, who went on to win the tournament. Sir Matt Busby, knighted in the New Year's Honours, retired at the end of the season.

Four-midable. Charlton seals the win

ROAD TO GLORY

LONDON

ZABRZE

SARAJEVO

MADRID

MALTA

Birthday Bliss. Brian Kidd, 19 on the day of the final, celebrates by scoring United's third

At last. United's legendary No 9 lifts the European Cup

Best in Europe

problems all season, watched the game from a hospital bed. Busby chose to use a 4-3-3 formation for the game, using the young Brian Kidd as a centre-forward between the two wingers John Aston and George Best. Crerand, Charlton and Sadler were stretched across the midfield with Brennan and Dunne chosen as full backs. Foulkes played in the middle of defence with Stiles designated to man-mark Eusebio and Stepney, as ever, in goal. Needless to say, the famous old stadium was filled to its 100,000 capacity, on an unusually hot and clammy May night.

The first half was scoreless, with both teams producing more graft than craft and the Italian referee whistling more than a beach-side building-site worker. Best was marked out of the game by two Portuguese defenders and Nobby Stiles had superglued himself to Eusebio. On 54 minutes, United broke the deadlock with a rare header from the famous pate of Bobby Charlton. They had several chances to put the game out of reach: goalkeeper Henrique saved at the feet of Aston then Best to keep the Portuguese in it. Then came a moment that silenced the crowd. With 78 minutes gone, Jaime equalised on the break, and suddenly it was all Benfica. Alex Stepney was magnificent, saving twice from Eusebio, who had suddenly come to life. On the second occasion the Mozambique-born attacker congratulated the keeper after he had cannonballed a shot into his midriff when a more delicate shot either side would have scored. Stepney's unwillingness to

Pat Crerand, Matt Busby and George Best parade the trophy amid high security

acknowledge this sportsmanship said a good deal about United's determination, though they looked like broken men when the 90-minute whistle finally went.

Busby's rallying words, however ("if you pass the ball to each other, you've got the beating of them"), rejuvenated the Blues and within ten minutes, unbelievably, United were 4–1 up. Best picked up a pass from Kidd and dribbled past the keeper to put United in front. Kidd – celebrating his 19th birthday – headed in the third, before Charlton swivelled to bang in the fourth and demoralise the Portuguese. In the dressing room afterwards veteran Bobby Charlton and manager Matt Busby were in tears, unable to speak. The tireless manager had finally reached the end of the rainbow he had been chasing for over a decade, and had spent all his emotional energy after the final whistle, running on the pitch in his black suit to celebrate with the team. The boys of '68 had achieved Busby's dream, though the boys of '58 – who surely would have already done so but for a cruel and tragic twist of fate – were doubtless never far from his mind.

Money matters

United were on a sliding scale of win bonuses in the 1968 European Cup. They won £50 per player for beating Hibernian of Malta and up to £1,000 (a fair amount of money in 1968) per player for winning the Final.

No room at the inn

United couldn't find a hotel in London for the night before the match and had to stay out in Berkshire.

MAN UNITED	4	BENFICA	1
	GOALS mins		GOALS mins
1 ALEX STEPNEY		1 HENRIQUE	
2 SHAY BRENNAN		2 ADOLFO	
3 TONY DUNNE		3 HUMBERTO	
4 PAT CRERAND		4 JACINTO	
5 BILL FOULKES		5 CRUZ	
6 NOBBY STILES		6 JAIME GRACA	78
7 GEORGE BEST	92	7 COLUNA	
8 BRIAN KIDD	95	8 JOSE AUGUSTO	
9 BOBBY CHARLTON	54, 101	9 TORRES	
10 DAVID SADLER		10 EUSEBIO	
11 JOHN ASTON		11 SIMOES	

CHAPTER **3**

The learning curve

Fergie's United in Europe

Long wait

After a terrible March 1993, Manchester United won the last seven matches of their season to cruise home and win the Premiership title. It was the first time United had finished top of the bunch since 1967 and the wild celebrations that followed in Manchester – and beyond – were due as much to relief as to unfettered joy. It was a particularly gratifying triumph for Alex Ferguson, who had arrived in 1986, picked the club up by the scruff of its neck, and now answered the many critics who had been calling for his head in 1989. But as he lifted the country's top trophy to the camera for the first time, you can bet your last Scottish pound that Ferguson had further ambitions in the back of his mind. The Premiership was sure to be the key to even further glory – entry into the European Cup competition – dizzy heights that United hadn't reached since they went out in the semi-final of the trophy they were defending in 1969.

It wasn't the manager's first foray into Europe. Ferguson had previously won the Cup-Winners' Cup with Aberdeen – against Real Madrid – in 1983. And, in 1991 (the first year that English clubs were allowed back into Europe after the five-year Heysel ban), United had done much to suggest that English teams would start where they had left off, when they beat Barcelona to win the European Cup-Winners' Cup.

The 1991 game was played on a balmy night in Rotterdam and was of particular importance to Mark Hughes, who had been dumped by the Spanish champions in 1987 before returning to Old Trafford. And it was the Welshman who won the game for the Reds (or, to be more accurate, the Whites) by scoring both of United's goals in their 2–1 win. The second was a brilliant thwack from a narrow angle after he rounded keeper Zubizaretta. The ball was hit with all the venom Hughes could muster against his former employees. United had beaten the great Barcelona side – comprising the likes of Koeman, Bakero and Stoichkov and

managed by Johan Cruyff – a team which went on to win the European Cup (Ferguson's ultimate target) a year later.

It was Ferguson's first European trophy win at Old Trafford. But, although United went on to become domestic kings in the '90s, the decade wasn't generally a happy one for them on the continent. United's European efforts in the two seasons between that 1991 win and their first foray into the European Cup in 1993 were singularly unsuccessful.

Their 1991/92 defence of the European Cup-Winners' Cup started with a whimper and ended in a bang. They managed a workaday 2–0 aggregate win over the Greek minnows Athinaikos in the first round, but came a cropper in the second against much stiffer opposition – Atletico Madrid. The tie started with a trip to Madrid and an embarrassing 3–0

Mark Hughes won the European Cup-Winn[er]'[s] Cup for United with goals against his for[mer] team, Barce[lona]

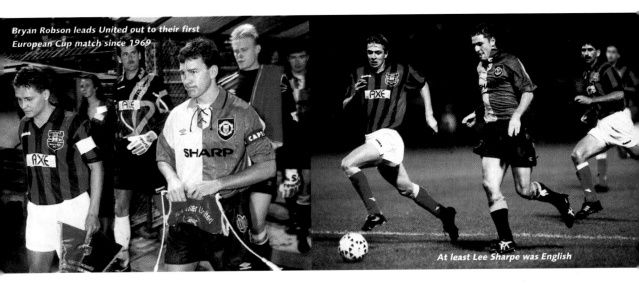

Bryan Robson leads United out to their first European Cup match since 1969

At least Lee Sharpe was English

defeat, which United never looked like turning over two weeks later at Old Trafford. A 1–1 draw was all they could muster. The following season, in the first round of the UEFA Cup, United were drawn against Torpedo Moscow (rather than the more illustrious Dynamo or Lokamotiv Moscow) and failed to score over two legs, both of which finished 0–0. They eventually went out on penalties in front of 11,300 in the Russian capital.

And so to 1993/94 and, at last, a crack at the biggest club trophy of them all. But Fergie's hands were tied by the five-foreigner rule, which meant that until 1996/97, he could never field his strongest team. Welsh, Scottish and Irish players were considered foreigners. Still, with their re-jigged team, United were drawn against Hungarian champions Kispest Honved, a team with years of European experience who nonetheless had never won one of the big three trophies. United virtually sealed the tie before half time of the first leg in Budapest, eventually winning 3–2 in front of 9,000 fans at the Jozsef Bozsik stadium. Playing in green and yellow, United went in front on just nine minutes with a cracking shot from £3.75million new boy Roy Keane who, like so many of his team-mates, was making his debut in the European Cup. Honved, crisp-passing and neat, pulled one back on 39 minutes, but a scintillating United scored twice just before the break – through Keane and Cantona – and, although they conceded a second before the end, they would have settled for the result before the game.

The return match, despite some stern warnings to his players by Ferguson, was something of a foregone conclusion – especially after Steve Bruce nodded United in front on 55 minutes. And it was the central defender, whose goals had done so much to get United into the competition, who added an identikit second ten minutes later and calmed even the most pessimistic home fan. Honved scored a late consolation goal, leaving most of the 35,871 fans who left the stadium happy that United had done the job rather than euphoric at the nature of the win.

United's victory put them into the second round and up against a team whose name every fan would soon know how to pronounce – Galatasaray from Istanbul. A quarter of the way though the season, champions United were virtually invincible in the Premiership; seven points clear of nearest rivals Norwich City (honest!) they looked even more unshakeable 13 minutes into the first leg of this European encounter at Old Trafford. At that point a Hakan Sukur own goal put United 2–0 up, Bryan Robson having opened the scoring with his first ever goal in Europe's premier competition on three minutes. Then someone let the air out of United's tyres and, 50 minutes later, Galatasaray were 3–2 up thanks to some brilliantly fluid football. Unbelievably, what had looked like a stroll in the park turned out to be sprint on broken glass as United battled to get something from the game – and maintain their 37-year-long invincible run at Old Trafford against European opposition. A late Eric Cantona strike did at least manage to save this proud record,

Two greats reunited

The Honved–United tie was watched by two former stars from the two teams' glory days, Bobby Charlton and Ferenc Puskas, who shook hands before the game in Budapest .

Goal hungry

Honved had been one of the great European sides of the '50s. Then, they provided most of the Hungarian team which beat England 6–3 at Wembley and 7–1 in Budapest, including Puskas, Koscic and Hidegkuti.

One Turkish banner read "Welcome to Hell". It summed up the whole atmosphere

but a brilliant performance in Turkey would be needed to get the team through.

The return in Istanbul, a fortnight later, was a game that United fans and players will never forget – though not for want of trying. United were met, as soon as they arrived from the airport, by intimidating, fanatical Galatasaray supporters and, when they made it to the ground, they were surrounded by 40,000 baying Ultras. One banner summed up the whole atmosphere. It read "Welcome to Hell". The noise (and Galatasaray's defensive and time-wasting tactics) were designed to put the Reds off their game, and it worked. United could hardly string two passes together and never looked like scoring. The match ended 0–0, the tie 3–3, and the whole fine mess was epitomised by a red card for Cantona after the whistle had sounded. United should never have put themselves into a position where, after being 2–0 up in the first leg, they needed to win in Turkey to get through. But, having gone out of the competition, at least they were able to get out of the country.

United's season was to end on a far brighter note, however, as their domestic superiority led to the club's first ever Double. They romped home eight points clear of Blackburn and thrashed Chelsea 4–0 in the Cup Final. The Premiership victory, of course, meant United qualified for the new format Champions' League, in which they went straight into the group stages of the competition. Still blighted by the five-foreigner rule, they were pitted against new opponents, Swedish champions Gothenburg, as well as old Euro foes Galatasaray and Barcelona. A home tie against Gothenburg kicked things off, and Old Trafford was stunned into silence (apart from the 250 Swedes who'd made the match) by a Stefan Pettersson goal on 27 minutes. However, United responded well in an exhilarating game, finishing the right side of a 4–2 scoreline, with Giggs bagging two goals.

We'll meet again. The Reds in action against Barcelona in 1994/95

Romario leaves the Reds looking on in awe

United stayed on track with another 0–0 draw at Istanbul's Ali Sami Yen stadium, which was less intimidating this time around. The same result, but a much better reward.

Next up was a double header against Barcelona. Brazilian World Cup hero Romario had joined Bakero, Koeman, Stoichkov *et al* at the Nou Camp in 1991, and now Barça were among the favourites to lift the trophy. But they looked second best at the start of the first tie at Old Trafford as United romped into an early lead thanks to the head of Mark Hughes. Then Cruyff's team went into top gear and scored a goal either side of half time to turn the game in their favour. It was United's turn to roll up their sleeves and pile on the pressure. It paid off. With ten minutes to go, Lee Sharpe scored a

Foreign legion

Alex Ferguson, bound by the ruling that no team could play more than five foreigners, had to leave Roy Keane out of the leg against Honved in what he called an 'agonising' decision. The 'foreigners' in the team were Schmeichel, Irwin, Cantona, Hughes and Giggs.

Cantona's Galatasaray 'hell'

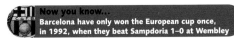

Now you know...
Barcelona have only won the European cup once, in 1992, when they beat Sampdoria 1–0 at Wembley

added a third to virtually put paid to United's Euro dreams for another season. United's final game in the group – a 4–0 victory over Galatasaray – was too little, too late, although it did avenge a score against the Turks.

It was a terrible year all round for United, who were pipped to the championship post by brawny Blackburn Rovers and beaten in the Cup Final by Everton – which meant that they only qualified for the UEFA Cup in the 1995/96 season. Once again, however, they failed in their task, going out to Rotor Volgograd on the away-goals rule. A young United side gained a valuable draw in Russia, but was sucker-punched at Old Trafford. There, 2–0 down after 24 minutes, they set themselves a target of three goals in the last hour but only managed two. The second, which at least saved their much-trumpeted 39-year unbroken home run in Europe, was a last-minute header by, of all people, Peter Schmeichel, who came up for a corner. The silver lining of yet another Euro-trashing was that United could now concentrate on the domestic scene and, sure enough, they won the Double again. They were the first team to do so twice, beating Newcastle United into second place and Liverpool in the FA Cup Final. The Premiership win meant another place in the Champions' League. With nothing left to prove in England, the stakes were getting higher if

brilliant equaliser, a cheeky back flick from a Cantona cross. It was a great European night, and United were looking forward to the return in the Nou Camp two weeks later.

It turned out to be a night everyone at United would rather forget. Stoichkov was superb and Gary Walsh (playing instead of Peter Schmeichel because of the five-foreigner rule) let in four goals as the Catalans put the English to the sword, making a mockery of their European dreams. Bad was to turn worse a fortnight later in Gothenburg. United were run ragged by a young player who was to feature strongly in their future: Jesper Blomqvist scored after just ten minutes. A Mark Hughes equaliser on 64 minutes was nullified seconds later by a second Swedish goal and Pontus Kamark

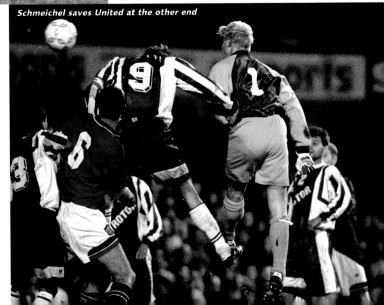

Schmeichel saves United at the other end

United wanted to prove themselves to be a truly great team. With the lifting of the five-foreigner rule at the start of the 1996/97 season, now was their chance.

United fans wanted to avoid Juventus in the Champions' League draw but, with two clubs qualifying out of four, they were quite happy that Rapid Vienna of Austria and Turkish side Fenerbahçe made up the numbers in their group. However United looked out of their league in their opening game against Eurochamps Juventus in Turin. Ferguson's tactic of playing Eric Cantona up front on his own with wing support from Jordi Cruyff and Karel Poborsky clearly failed, and United were overrun in midfield. The wonder was that Juventus didn't score more than their solitary goal, notched up by Croat Alen Boksic.

To restore their shattered confidence United needed an easy game at home. Rapid Vienna fitted the bill. The Austrians rarely ventured into the United half and goals by Solskjaer and Beckham in the first half hour enabled fans to go home with their fingernails intact. Three weeks on, United improved their position in the group with a classy win over Fenerbahçe in Turkey. The Reds rode the Turkish storm in the first half, silenced the crowd and scored two second-half goals – through Beckham and Cantona – to wrap up the game. It was like watching the Liverpool of old.

It seemed now that only a disaster could threaten United's route to the quarter-finals, what with two home matches on the trot and that famous unbeaten-at-home record now stretching back 40 years. But disaster struck. United scorned chance after chance against Fenerbahçe, who scored a late crowd-silencing goal through their Bosnian striker Bolic to take the points. And three weeks later, fortress Old Trafford was breached again, this time by Juventus. Butt brought down Del Piero in the box and the international striker picked himself up to score the penalty on 35 minutes. An exciting second-half cavalry charge by United was in vain. Though the players in red were heroes to a man, they fell to their third defeat in the group and slipped into third spot.

A win in Vienna was vital on a bitterly cold

night in Austria, where the temperature was a more Siberian –12°C. Early on in the game, Schmeichel produced an unforgettable save that many ranked alongside that of Gordon Banks' against Pele in the 1970 World Cup. Rene Wagner rose to head the ball into the net but Schmeichel leapt to his right and somehow contrived to knock the ball over the bar. It was a let-off that Rapid were to rue. On 24 minutes, United scored a goal to match the Great Dane's save. Giggs, on the halfway line, found Cantona, who returned the favour with a defence-splitting ball that the Welshman drove past the keeper. Half way through the second half Cantona slid in on a Beckham cross to double the score and put Fergie's men into the quarter-final draw.

Porto came out of the hat, with the first leg at Old Trafford. Rarely has that great stadium seen such a stunning exhibition of football. United tore the Portuguese champions apart with consummate ease. Surprisingly, David May scored the first, prodding the ball in from close range. Cantona scored a second in the first half and Giggs and Cole completed the rout. United might have sat back at 2–0, worried about an away goal, but to their credit they pressed home their advantage, ensuring a semi-final place – barring an absolute disaster in Porto.

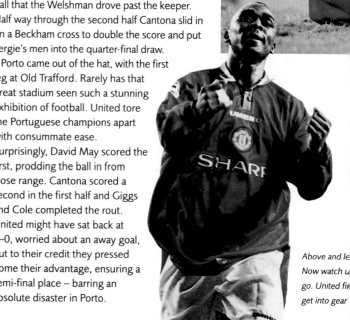

Above and le
Now watch u
go. United fir
get into gear

Now you know...
Borussia Dortmund's star player in the 1996/97 Champions'
League was the little-known Scotsman Paul Lambert

So near... United fall at the semi-final hurdle against Dortmund

help of a Gary Pallister deflection. Now United needed three goals to win the tie. The crowd's confidence ebbed as the United players created chances but just couldn't put them away and, before long, their task became impossible. Dortmund were through to the final against Juventus. How United would have loved to be in their place – especially as the venue was Munich, scene of the tragic air crash 29 years before. Still, having lost three times at Old Trafford in the competition, with a total record of played ten, won four, drawn one and lost five, many argued that they didn't actually deserve to be in the final anyway.

Yet again, however, United prevailed at home where they had failed abroad and another Premiership trophy in the coffers meant another berth in the Champions' League. United cursed their luck to be drawn against Juventus again for the 1997/98 campaign, but were happy with the other two teams in their group – Feyenoord and the Slovakians FC Kosice.

United's first hurdle was the trip to Eastern Europe, and they sauntered over it with a 3–0 win in a stadium that wouldn't have looked out of place in the Vauxhall Conference. Irwin put United in front on the half hour, Berg doubled the score on the hour and Cole kept things symmetrical by notching a third just before the final whistle. It was a morale-boosting start to the campaign – and it was needed: Juventus were due at Old Trafford for the next game.

Within an incredible 19 seconds, the Italians were in front. Del Piero meandered through a

But a disaster never looked on the cards a fortnight later, as a composed United kept their third consecutive clean sheet away from home in the tournament. For the first time since 1969, United had reached the semi-final of the European Cup.

Borussia Dortmund were the opponents, and the first leg was played in Germany in front of 48,500 noisy fans. For 73 minutes United out-played their hosts but couldn't find the target. Then Cantona lost the ball in midfield, René Tretschok cracked in a shot, and United were behind. They were never to get level again.

Just eight minutes were on the clock in the Old Trafford leg of the game when Lars Ricken stole into the box and beat Schmeichel with the

Eric Cantona lost the ball in midfield, René Tretschok cracked in a shot, and United were behind. They were never to get level again

defence that were bodily present but mentally still in the dressing room, to stun the 53,000 fans in the stadium. They were to remain stunned all game as United fought back against this mishap, relentlessly tearing at the Juventus defence to try to get back in the game. And get back they did, scoring three times (through Sheringham, Scholes and Giggs) to dispel any notions of Italian invincibility. Although Zidane pulled a goal back on the final whistle, it was

United who gained all the plaudits on a night no Reds fan will ever forget. Quite simply, United looked champion.

Two games against Feyenoord followed, the first at Old Trafford. United's finishing let them down on the night, and what should have been a rout finished nervily after Henk Vos scored a late goal to put the Dutch within catching distance. United had scored through Scholes and Irwin. But there were no such nerves in the De Kuip stadium, resulting in a superb Andy Cole hat-trick. Feyenoord did manage a late reply but the goal was less damaging to United than Paul Bosvelt's studs, which were viciously stamped into Denis Irwin's calf as tempers frayed. Four games and four wins – this was more like it.

A fifth consecutive victory, at home to Kosice, qualified Alex Ferguson's team for the quarter-finals. They immediately became bookies' favourites to lift the trophy. Cole scored on 40 minutes, but that was all that separated the sides until a couple of late ones

Hose sorry now?
Alex Ferguson instructed his groundsmen to water the Old Trafford pitch before the Monaco game in order to try to slow down the quick-footed Frenchmen.

Above: United come of age in Europe with a famous win over Juve

Below: Andrew Cole puts three past Feyenoord

(an own goal and a Sheringham strike) made the scoreline something more like what everyone had been expecting. All that was left on the agenda was a meaningless trip to Juventus – a weakened United team defended their goal successfully for 83 minutes, then Inzaghi scored. But thanks to a last-minute Olimpiakos equaliser against Rosenborg, the Old Lady snuck into the quarter-finals through the back door.

United drew French champs Monaco in the quarter-final, and acquitted themselves well in the first leg in the weird cabbage-patch stadium in Monte Carlo. They came away with a draw after a stultifyingly boring defensive performance which nearly saw French keeper Barthez fall asleep in the second half. The result looked good until five minutes into the second leg at Old Trafford, when Trezeguet broke away to score a belter against Rai Van Der Gouw. Solskjaer raised hopes with an equaliser on 53 minutes, but the French defence were as effective in England as United's had been in France, and – again, frustratingly – Barthez had virtually nothing to do as United couldn't turn their pressure into clear-cut chances.

Thirty years on from the 1968 win, and 40 years on from the Munich air disaster, United had failed to win the European Champions' League – again.

CHAPTER **4**

The first hurdle

United invade Poland to dislodge Lodz

Two teams, Poles apart

QUALIFYING ROUND First Leg | 12 August 1998 | Old Trafford | Att: 50,906 | Ref: A Quzounov (Bulgaria) | Entertainment: 50%

Manchester United 2 Lodz 0 United: Cole, Giggs

One of the consequences of not winning the title in 1998 was that United, who qualified for the Champions' League by finishing in second place in the Premiership, had to go through a preliminary round before being drawn in the Champions' League proper. They were drawn against Polish champions LKS Lodz, who had beaten Kepev Ganja (from Azerbaijan, not Jamaica) 7–2 in a preliminary round.

Internal disputes, however, within the Polish FA introduced the mouthwatering possibility of United being given a bye through to the group stage as UEFA threatened to expel all Polish clubs from competitions after 33 members of the Polish FA had been sacked by the Sports minister Jacek Debski. However, Debski negotiated a last-minute reprieve, which saw Lodz scheduled to play at Old Trafford on 12 August

(three days after the Charity Shield defeat by Arsenal) and in Poland just two weeks later.

Ferguson, of course, had sent scouts to see Lodz's preliminary games against Kepev, but he didn't receive a video of the matches until a day before the Old Trafford game, so he wasn't able to prepare his players fully for the match. Lodz's players were virtually unknown to him as there were very few internationals in the team, and their two foreigners, Rodrigo Carbone of Brazil and Omadiagbe Darlington of Nigeria, were hardly household names. Miroslaw Trzerciak, who had scored four goals for the Polish side in the previous qualifier, had recently left for Osasuna in Spain.

The Poles, already a commentator's nightmare because of their long, consonant-filled names (there's only one Zbibniew Wyciszkiewicz!) made life in the gantry even more difficult by shaving their heads to a man. For this they received £2,000 (a lotta zloty) from their main

Russian around

LKS Lodz started life as a Russian club – in 1908 Poland did not exist as a sovereign state.

Lodzamoney!

LKS stands for Lodski Klub Sportowy (Sporting Club of Lodz) although since 1994 the official title of the club has been LKS Ptak Lodz after a local businessman, Antoni Ptak, who saved the club from bankruptcy.

MANCHESTER UNITED					2
HOME TEAM	GOALS mins	ASSISTS mins	SHOTS ON	OFF	SUB'D mins
1 PETER SCHMEICHEL					
2 GARY NEVILLE			1		
5 RONNY JOHNSEN					
6 JAAP STAM			1	2	
3 DENIS IRWIN		80		2	
7 DAVID BECKHAM			3	2	
16 ROY KEANE			1		
8 NICKY BUTT					
11 RYAN GIGGS	15		2	2	
18 PAUL SCHOLES		15	1		81
9 ANDREW COLE	80		4	2	

SUBSTITUTES	GOALS mins	ASSISTS mins	SHOTS ON	OFF	SUB'D for
31 NICK CULKIN					
12 PHIL NEVILLE					
14 JORDI CRUYFF					
20 OLE GUNNAR SOLSKJAER					#18
10 TEDDY SHERINGHAM					
4 DAVID MAY					
21 HENNING BERG					

MATCH STATS
SHOTS ON TARGET 10 FOULS 15 OFFSIDES 1
SHOTS OFF TARGET 13 FREE KICKS 14 CORNER KICKS 0
UNITED'S RATING 70%

LKS LODZ					0
AWAY TEAM	GOALS mins	ASSISTS mins	SHOTS ON	OFF	SUB'D mins
1 BOGUSLAW WYPARLO					
7 RAFAL PAWLAK					
4 WITOLD BENDKOWSKI			1		
6 GRZEGORZ KRYSIAK					
16 OMADIAGBE DARLINGTON					85
25 TOMASZ CEBULA					
19 ZBIBNIEW WYCISZKIEWICZ					
3 TOMASZ KOS			1		
9 RAFAL NIZNIK			1		57
33 TOMASZ WIESZCZYKI					
8 DZIDOSLAW ZUBEREK			1		72

SUBSTITUTES	GOALS mins	ASSISTS mins	SHOTS ON	OFF	SUB'D for
20 JACEK PLUCIENNIK					
15 RODRIGO					#9
17 ARIEL JAKUBOWSKI					#16
2 PASZULEWICZ					#8
12 MICHAEL SLAWATA					
23 ARTUR BUGAJ					
21 PIOTR					

MATCH STATS
SHOTS ON TARGET 1 FOULS 14 OFFSIDES 0
SHOTS OFF TARGET 3 FREE KICKS 15 CORNER KICKS 0
LKS'S RATING 28%

Cole – axed

sponsors, Atlas, the manufacturers of a glue designed to keep wigs on heads.

Before the game Alex Ferguson said that he would settle for a 1–0 win. "The main thing is that we don't lose a goal. If you win 1–0 at home in Europe you always have a chance," he stated, though it is likely he expected a little more from his players. However, he must have been aware that three years earlier English champions Blackburn Rovers were surprisingly knocked out of the competition by Polish champs Legia Warsaw and that United had to guard carefully against complacency.

United, and Ryan Giggs in particular, began looking like they could wrap up the tie in the first 15 minutes. Giggs, who had missed the previous year's agonising quarter-final exit to Monaco with a hamstring injury, was back to his scintillating best and had a chance as early as the fourth minute when Polish keeper Wyparlo punched a cross clear off

> 66 **The difference between United and LKS is the same as the difference between Heathrow and Lodz airports** 99
>
> FORMER LODZ GOALKEEPER AND COACH JAN TOMACZEWSKI

his head. Shortly afterwards he blasted a shot straight at the keeper, then found his range with a left-foot shot into the Polish net. It was exactly the breathing space United needed.

However the fact that United needed another class striker – in a week in which the Dwight Yorke deal seemed dead – became apparent as they failed to capitalise on their lead. Cole was particularly wasteful of the sort of chances he should have taken in his sleep and Beckham was unusually inaccurate with a series of free kicks. Then, with less than ten minutes left and the Old Trafford crowd becoming increasingly frustrated, United virtually put themselves in the next round with a second goal, Cole finally coming good. Giggs sent Irwin on a run which ended with a cut-in from the bye-line which the No 9 powerfully headed in from ten yards.

"LKS were so frightened that even if their they had been ordered to go forward they couldn't have," said their former goalkeeper and coach Jan Tomaczewski (who broke English hearts back in 1973 at Wembley) afterwards. "The difference between United and LKS is the same as the difference between Heathrow and Lodz airports."

Pole position

LKS had made one other appearance in the European Cup, in 1959/60, and were knocked out in the first round by minnows Jeunesse Esch, winning 2–1 in Poland but losing 5–0 in Luxembourg.

Red mist

United's only previous encounter against a team from Lodz saw them go out of the UEFA Cup in 1980/81 to Widsew Lodz on away goals after a 1–1 draw at Old Trafford and a scoreless return in Poland.

United cruise through...

QUALIFYING ROUND Second Leg | 26 August 1998 | LKS Stadium | Att: 8,000 | Ref: VC Graziano (Italy) | Entertainment: 50%

LKS Lodz 0 Manchester United 0

United's task of not losing 3–0 in Poland was helped by behind-the-scenes disarray at LKS Lodz before the return game. Brazilian striker Rodrigo Carbone's huffy return home after a pay dispute and a fans' embargo on the game over increased ticket prices (double the normal rate at £6) didn't help the Poles' near-impossible task of beating United at least 2–0, despite the fact that United's own start to the season had been little more than mediocre (2–2 at home to Leicester City and 0–0 at West Ham United).

The Poles' attacking ambitions, however, had increased – as had their hair length – and they showed early on that they did, after all, know how to operate in the opponents' half. Just 25 seconds had elapsed when Rafal Niznik nipped in front of Denis Irwin and popped a 25-yarder just wide of the post. Gradually, however, with

Roy Keane outstanding in midfield and Stam and Johnsen impenetrable in the centre of defence, United stifled the East European threat and took over the game with a display of discipline and determination that had neutral TV viewers switching over channels in their droves and United fans in the stands and at home chatting among themselves. And it was United who looked the likelier team to score, the best chances falling to Sheringham, who hit a Giggs cross wide, Keane, with a vicious 30-yarder, Beckham whose dipper was touched over the bar by the competent Polish keeper, and Solskjaer, thwarted by Wyparlo in the closing stages of the game.

If this was just a stroll in a foreign park for United, it was an important one, with a place in the Champions' League up for grabs, and all the glamour and profit that goes with it assured. The only real blot in the copybook was Beckham's booking for a needless foul.

Nice little earner
Qualifying for the Champions' League proper was worth at least £5million to Manchester United in extra gate receipts, TV money, advertising and sponsorship revenue. Getting to the Final netted the club an estimated total of £15million.

LKS LODZ					0
HOME TEAM	GOALS mins	ASSISTS mins	SHOTS ON	OFF	SUB'D mins
1 BOGUSLAW WYPARLO					
7 RAFAL PAWLAK					
4 WITOLD BENDKOWSKI					
6 GRZEGORZ KRYSIAK					
17 ARIEL JAKUBOWSKI					84
3 TOMASZ KOS			1		
19 ZBIBNIEW WYCISZKIEWICZ					
5 T LENART					81
9 RAFAL NIZNIK			1		
33 TOMASZ WIESZCZYKI					
8 DZIDOSLAW ZUBEREK					51

SUBSTITUTES	GOALS mins	ASSISTS mins	SHOTS ON	OFF	SUB'D for
21 P MATYS					#8
20 JACEK PLUCIENNIK					#5
23 ARTUR BUGAJ					#17
2 PASZULEWICZ					
12 MICHAEL SLAWATA					

MATCH STATS
SHOTS ON TARGET 1 | FOULS 11 | OFFSIDES 3
SHOTS OFF TARGET 1 | FREE KICKS 14 | CORNER KICKS 2
LKS'S RATING 39%

MANCHESTER UNITED					0
AWAY TEAM	GOALS mins	ASSISTS mins	SHOTS ON	OFF	SUB'D mins
1 PETER SCHMEICHEL					
12 PHIL NEVILLE					
5 RONNY JOHNSEN			1		
6 JAAP STAM					
3 DENIS IRWIN					
7 DAVID BECKHAM			1	1	
16 ROY KEANE			1		
8 NICKY BUTT			1	1	
11 RYAN GIGGS			1		64
10 TEDDY SHERINGHAM			1		
18 PAUL SCHOLES					

SUBSTITUTES	GOALS mins	ASSISTS mins	SHOTS ON	OFF	SUB'D for
4 DAVID MAY					
9 ANDY COLE					
13 RAI VAN DER GOUW					
20 OLE GUNNAR SOLSKJAER			1		#11
14 JORDI CRUYFF					
30 WES BROWN					
21 HENNING BERG					

MATCH STATS
SHOTS ON TARGET 4 | FOULS 14 | OFFSIDES 2
SHOTS OFF TARGET 5 | FREE KICKS 11 | CORNER KICKS 5
UNITED'S RATING 57%

It seemed like a good idea at the time...

If this was a stroll in a foreign park for United, it was an important one, with a place in the Champions' League up for grabs

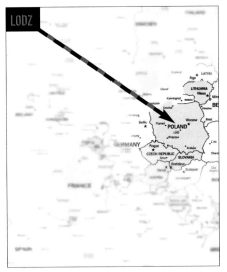

LODZ

POLAND

Wot, no Yorke?

Aston Villa turned down a final offer for their striker Dwight Yorke on the day of the first leg against Lodz — then sold him on the day of the return for £12.6 million, a record for both clubs.

Where on Earth?

Lodz, a textile-producing industrial city in central Poland, is the country's second largest city with a population of just under a million (twice that of Manchester). Dating back to 500, AD Lodz boasts not one but two universities.

"The group of death"

The draw for the Champions' League group stage, which took place in Monte Carlo on 27 August, had made Alex Ferguson and his players roll their sleeves up in anticipation of the tough fights ahead of them

United's Group D was immediately nicknamed 'the group of death' as it contained three giants, United, Bayern Munich and Barcelona, as well as dark horses Brondby, making it by far the toughest of the six. Munich, of course, had huge symbolic value to United who hadn't played a competitive match there since the air disaster in 1958. Barcelona had seen Ferguson's young team thrashed 4–0 four years before, which did much to demoralise his European ambitions. The good news was that Brondby, Peter Schmeichel's former team, had lost 6–0 to the Reds in a pre-season friendly.

Automatic English qualifiers Arsenal found that their task wasn't much easier: they were placed in Group E, alongside French champions Lens, Greek champs Panathinaikos and Dynamo Kiev, who had scraped through the qualifiers against Sparta Prague after losing the first leg at home. Group C looked tough, too, with Ronaldo's Inter paired against Champions' League holders Real Madrid, and Russian champs Spartak Moscow and Austrians Sturm Graz making up the numbers. Last years' losing finalists Juventus were paired with Athletic Bilbao, who had finished third in the Spanish League, as well as Galatasaray (who United were pleased to avoid) and Rosenborg of Norway. Graeme Souness' Portuguese qualifiers Benfica weren't too daunted by finding themselves grouped in with Stamless PSV Eindhoven, Helsinki and unfashionable German champions Kaiserslautern.

Finally, the easiest group looked to be Group A, where Ajax seemed certain to qualify against Porto, Olimpiakos and Croatia Zagreb. At the time, anyway. . .

Welsh win!

Most of the smaller nations' teams had to participate in the first qualifying phase. The only team from this phase to make it to the group stages were Ukranian champs Dynamo Kiev. They beat Welsh Barry Town 10–1 on aggregate in July.

How they qualified...

Porto, Ajax, Barcelona, Juventus, Lens, Arsenal and Kaiserslautern all qualified automatically as champions. Real Madrid qualified as holders. The others, like United, had to fight their way through in the qualifiers. Here are the results of the second qualifying phase (qualifiers in bold)

QUALIFYING ROUND

Rosenborg v Club Brugge
2–0 2–4 (Rosenborg win on away goals)

Manchester United v LKS Lodz
2–0 0–0 (United win 2–0)

FC Liteks v Spartak Moscow
0–5 2–6 (Spartak win 11–2)

Galatasaray v Grasshoppers
2–1 3–2 (Galatasaray win 5–3)

Celtic v Croatia Zagreb
1–0 0–3 (Croatia win 3–1)

Maribor v PSV Eindhoven
2–1 1–4 (PSV win 5–3)

Dynamo Kiev v Sparta Prague
0–1 1–0 (Kiev win 3–1 on pens)

Kosice v Brondby
0–2 1–0 (Brondby win 2–1)

Inter Milan v FC Skonto
4–0 3–1 (Inter win 7–1)

Olimpiakos v Anorthosis
2–1 4–2 (Olimpiakos win 6–3)

Benfica v Beitar Jerusalem
6–0 2–4 (Benfica win 8–4)

Dynamo Tblisi v Athletic Bilbao
2–1 0–1 (Bilbao win on away goals)

HJK Helsinki v FC Metz
1–0 1–1 (Helsinki win 2–1)

Bayern Munich v FK Obilic
4–0 1–1 (Bayern Munich win 5–1)

Sturm Graz v Ujpesti
4–0 3–2 (Sturm Graz win 7–2)

Steaua Bucharest v Panathinaikos
2–2 3–6 (Panathinaikos win 8–5)

Group A
AJAX AMSTERDAM
PORTO FC
OLIMPIAKOS PIRAEUS
CROATIA ZAGREB

Group B
JUVENTUS
ATHLETIC BILBAO
ROSENBORG
GALATASARAY

Group C
REAL MADRID
INTER MILAN
STURN GRAZ
SPARTAK MOSCOW

Group D
BARCELONA
MANCHESTER UNITED
BAYERN MUNICH
BRONDBY

Group E
LENS
ARSENAL
PANATHINAIKOS
DYNAMO KIEV

Group F
KAISERSLAUTERN
PSV EINDHOVEN
BENFICA
HJK HELSINKI

CHAPTER **5**

Let the games begin...

Manchester United enter the group of death

To Catalan story short...

Manchester United 3 Barcelona 3 United: Giggs, Scholes, Beckham Barcelona: Anderson, Giovanni, Luis Enrique

As we've seen, Champions' League Group D was immediately dubbed 'the group of death' as it contained three of Europe's top teams – Barcelona, Bayern Munich and, of course, Manchester United, as well as Danish wild cards Brondby. United effectively faced a sudden death situation in their first game when they were paired against Barcelona at Old Trafford. It was highly important to win this match as it was widely predicted, that with sides taking points off each other, only one team was likely to qualify from the group (see 'The rules', opposite).

As the Spanish season doesn't kick off until September, Barcelona hardly had a chance to get into gear, with only two unimpressive performances in their league and defeat against minnows Mallorca in the Spanish Super Cup (the equivalent of the Charity Shield) behind them. Dutch coach Louis van Gaal (a former PE teacher nicknamed 'The Nutty Professor') was under huge pressure from the Spanish press (Rottweilers who make our hacks look like poodles) to succeed. Even though Barça had won the League and Cup Double under van Gaal in the preceding season, arch-rivals Real Madrid had bagged the big one, the European Cup, to eclipse their glory. And did the Catalans not like that.

What's more, Barça were bereft of key players, particularly in defence, including the impressive Miguel Nadal – once a subject of United interest – (out with a muscle strain) and Winston Bogarde. Also out injured were Josep Guardiola, who tore United's midfield to shreds in 1994, Emmanuel Amunike and Albert Celades, with new signings Patrick Kluivert and Mauricio Pellegrino ineligible. But the Barcelona team still included the likes of Brazilians Rivaldo, Sonny Anderson and Giovanni, their Portuguese skipper Luis Figo, Spanish internationals Luis Enrique and Sergi and Dutchmen Ruud Hesp, Michael Reiziger,

Philip Cocu and Bolo Zenden. For their part, United were at full strength apart from Ronny Johnsen, but they had Henning Berg to step in.

Both managers had been doing their homework on the opposition, but United had a singular advantage, with two 'spies' in their camp. Jaap Stam knew all about his World Cup colleagues Reiziger, Cocu and Zenden while Jordi Cruyff had grown up at Barcelona, where his dad Johan had been coach, and had come through the club's youth programme to star in the first team before moving to United.

Before the game, Fergie urged United's supporters to make more noise than usual. He needn't have bothered. United's start was so exhilarating that even the press box was up and cheering. As early as the tenth minute United should have had a goal. A visionary cross-field Beckham pass not only found Giggs, but found him in space, a good yard ahead of his marker

The rules...

The two best runners-up from the six Champions' League groups were scheduled to get through to the quarter-finals, along with the six group winners, according to points scored and goal difference records.

> **Some people are calling it the group of death, but I didn't even consider that. These games are what the Champions' League is all about**
>
> ALEX FERGUSON

A night for big hearts

" Trying to emulate Busby's 1968 success has become an albatross around my neck. All that domestic success will be regarded as failure if we don't win the European Cup "

ALEX FERGUSON

Getting ready to rumble

" You need a strong squad of at least 20 to compete at home and in Europe. I think we've got that now " ALEX FERGUSON

(strangely, the attacking midfielder Luis Enrique). Giggs found Solskjaer in the box and the little Norwegian flashed a shot from six yards – onto the bar. Then Ryan Giggs, who started splendidly, beat Luis Figo on the left and crossed in again, only for Yorke to head the ball over the bar. But a goal looked inevitable, with United's tenacious midfield pressing Barcelona into unaccustomed errors and, once they had the ball, belting upfield with quick passes and quicker legs. And on 17 minutes it came; Yorke's pass found Beckham, who outwitted and outpaced Sergi before hitting a superb swerving diagonal cross from the right. Ryan Giggs jumped higher than the hapless Luis Enrique to head in a thumping centre-forward-type header, despite the fact that the ball was slightly behind him. It was a classic English goal, akin to the brace scored by Tino Asprilla for Newcastle against the same opposition a year earlier in the same competition.

And that was not all. On 24 minutes, a mixture of team-work, flair and persistence led to a second United goal. Beckham, who had found his perfect crossing range, again whipped the ball in from the right. This time Dwight Yorke was on the end of it with a flamboyant and athletic scissor kick. Hesp saved bravely, though more through luck than judgement, and the ball bounced off Luis Enrique, who was looking increasingly out of position at right back. Scholes, with a late run into the box, was on hand to snaffle up the rebound, and United were in dreamland.

United continued pouring forward, the wind in their sails being blown by the raucous Old Trafford crowd, who were enjoying having a go at Patrick Kluivert, sitting in the stands, with such songs as, "Patrick, Patrick, what's the score?" and "You should have signed for a big club." Kluivert had spurned an offer to play for United in the summer to move to Barcelona, and he hadn't been forgiven.

The one man who was pleased about that in Manchester (give or take one Andrew Cole) was Ole Gunnar Solskjaer, who was at hand to

White Reds

United played in white at Old Trafford instead of their customary red because Barcelona, confused about the Champions' League rulings, turned up at Old Trafford with only one kit – their clashing red and blue.

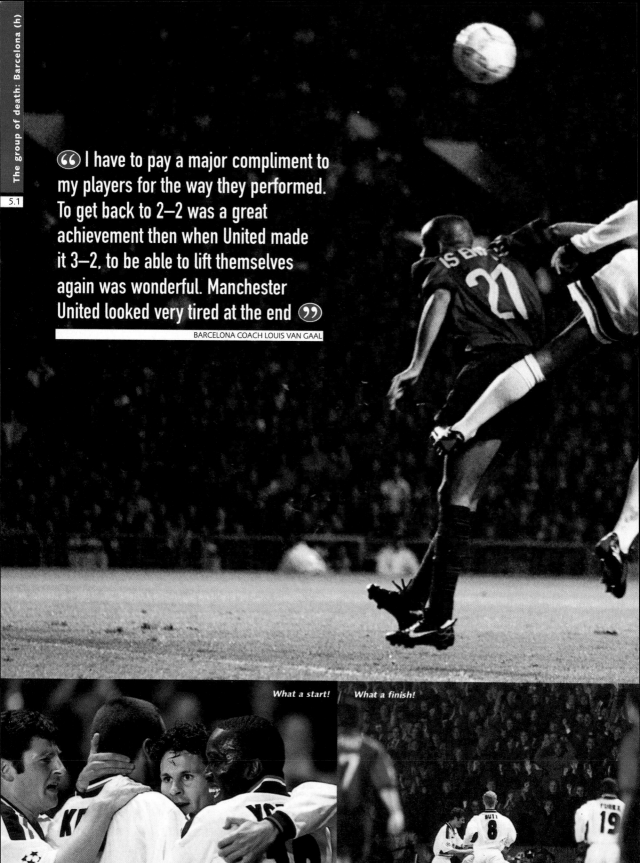

66 I have to pay a major compliment to my players for the way they performed. To get back to 2–2 was a great achievement then when United made it 3–2, to be able to lift themselves again was wonderful. Manchester United looked very tired at the end **99**

BARCELONA COACH LOUIS VAN GAAL

What a start!

What a finish!

What a choker!

Now you know...
In 17 visits to British clubs, Barcelona have
only won once – at Wolves in 1960

pounce after Hesp had fumbled a shot from
Gary Neville midway through the half.
Unbelievably, with the Norwegian poised to
score, referee Stefano Braschi – a commercial
agent from Italy – blew his whistle, calling the
striker up for a foul only he had seen. It was his
first major mistake of the evening.

But by no means his last. After an
exhilarating first half hour,
United understandably went
off the boil, which allowed
Barcelona to compose
themselves and rally. On 34
minutes Rivaldo, so far
virtually anonymous,
scored a rasper (via a Paul
Scholes deflection) to put
Barça back into the
game. Or so he
thought. Braschi
disallowed the
goal for an (as it
turned out
non-existent)
offside on Sonny
Anderson. Suddenly it
was all Barcelona – only a brilliant point-blank
save by Peter Schmeichel thwarted another
effort by van Gaal's men. United were relieved
when Braschi blew the half-time whistle – though
not half as relieved as they would be an hour later.
  Barcelona started the second half as they had
ended the first, with Luis Enrique unshackled
from his defensive duties and suddenly looking
like a world-class, rather than a Sunday-league,
footballer. United, attempting to sit on their
lead, were trying to play the ball through their
full backs instead of working in the Barcelona
half, and the Spanish team were thriving on the

**❝ The first penalty was a
disgrace. There was no contact
and unfortunately for us it
gave Barcelona greater impetus
at an important time ❞**

ALEX FERGUSON

MANCHESTER UNITED — 3

HOME TEAM	GOALS mins	ASSISTS mins	SHOTS ON	OFF	SUB'D mins
1 PETER SCHMEICHEL					
2 GARY NEVILLE					
3 DENIS IRWIN					79
6 JAAP STAM					
21 HENNING BERG					
16 ROY KEANE				1	
18 PAUL SCHOLES	24			1	
7 DAVID BECKHAM	64	17	1	1	
11 RYAN GIGGS	17		1	1	84
20 OLE GUNNAR SOLSKJAER				2	55
19 DWIGHT YORKE				1	

SUBSTITUTES	GOALS mins	ASSISTS mins	SHOTS ON	OFF	SUB'D for
17 RAI VAN DER GOUW					
4 DAVID MAY					
8 ▌NICKY BUTT					#20
9 ANDREW COLE					
10 TEDDY SHERINGHAM					
12 PHIL NEVILLE					#3
15 JESPER BLOMQVIST					#11

MATCH STATS
SHOTS ON TARGET 5 FOULS 16 OFFSIDES 2
SHOTS OFF TARGET 4 FREE KICKS 5 CORNER KICKS 2
UNITED'S RATING 82%

extra space they were finding. Two minutes after the restart and Rivaldo muscled his way into the United box somehow, via two rebounds off defenders, got the ball through to his compatriot Sonny Anderson, who found space and time to curl it left-footed past Schmeichel. It has to be said, it was no less than the Catalans deserved.

Worse was to follow. On the hour Jaap Stam made a foolish lunge at Rivaldo in the box. Though contact was minimal, the Brazilian dived like he'd been shot. To a chorus of boos, Giovanni belted the ball in from the spot: 2–2 and half an hour to go.

Three minutes later fortune smiled on United. Giovanni, still glowing from his goal, fouled Yorke just outside the box – Beckham territory. Becks bent a dipping curler over the wall and into the top left-hand corner of the net, with Hesp easily beaten. It was a brilliant strike,

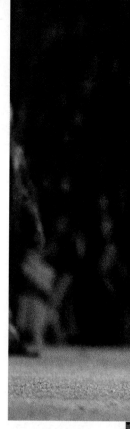

> ❝ If it is handball then it is handball, but when the ball hits the hand of a man who is on the line, then I think that is where the decision becomes very harsh. We were penalised on both counts there, losing a player and a goal ❞ ALEX FERGUSON

BARCELONA — 3

AWAY TEAM	GOALS mins	ASSISTS mins	SHOTS ON	OFF	SUB'D mins
13 RUUD HESP					
2 MICHAEL REIZIGER			1		
12 SERGI BARJUAN					
5 ALBERLADO FERNANDEZ					
21 LUIS ENRIQUE MARTINEZ	71		1	1	
15 PHILIP COCU					
7 LUIS FIGO			4		
23 BOLO ZENDEN					
11 RIVALDO		47	2	3	
10 GIOVANNI DE OLIVERA	60		2	1	68
9 SONNY ANDERSON	47		2	2	

SUBSTITUTES	GOALS mins	ASSISTS mins	SHOTS ON	OFF	SUB'D for
1 VITOR BAIA					
6 OSCAR GARCIA					
16 DRAGAN CIRIC					
22 GBENGA OKUNOWO					
24 ROGER GARCIA					
26 XAVI HERNANDEZ CRUZ					#10

MATCH STATS
SHOTS ON TARGET 7 FOULS 5 OFFSIDES 5
SHOTS OFF TARGET 12 FREE KICKS 16 CORNER KICKS 6
BARCA'S RATING 79%

strongly reminiscent of his World Cup goal against Colombia in Lens, and United's celebrations, with Beckham sitting on the touchline, fists clenched and all his team-mates piled on top of him, are almost as hard to forget as the goal itself. But it turned out to be United's last positive contribution of the match.

The Reds, who had started the game so full of energy, were starting to look tired, and if the Barcelona midfield had found it difficult to find space in the first half hour, they had all the time in the world on the ball in the last. Keane was looking far from match-fit and Scholes like a young man with World Cup fatigue. But instead of substituting either of these with the fresh and willing Butt, Ferguson brought on the United No 8 for Solskjaer to bolster his midfield.

He wasn't to stay on the field long. On 70 minutes Luis Enrique outwitted his first-half tormentor Giggs and Irwin, too, and hit a cross into the box that the ever-willing Anderson headed against the bar. The ball fell into the

No sooner on than off: Butt has to go

The referee had a shocker, a real shocker! I saw the Barcelona president go into the referee's room after the game. I'm sure he was delighted to see him

ALEX FERGUSON

Owned by the Pope

Much of the newspaper coverage, both back and front pages, at the time of the game concerned United's acceptance of Rupert Murdoch's £623million offer for the club. This was in sharp contrast to Barcelona's situation. The Catalan club is effectively owned by their 112,000 members (including the Pope!) whose subscription fees are used to pay players' transfer fees and wages.

mixer – Zenden hit a shot which rebounded to Anderson who blasted goalwards from close range. Butt, who had tracked back to the goal-line, instinctively stuck his arm out (or did it just hit it?) and Figo netted the rebound. Inexplicably, however, Braschi disallowed the goal and pointed to the spot, which meant that Butt had to go and the redhead was duly red-carded off the field. Luis Enrique, with Giovanni having been substituted, knocked the ball in and United had lost both a man and a goal.

The last 20 minutes were all Barcelona, who ended the game showing the same aggression with which United had started. But somehow, through a combination of last-gasp defending and Schmeichel agility (Big Pete, at least, wasn't knackered) United held out for a point, which, unbelievably after the glory of the first half hour, they were extremely grateful for. Next up Bayern, who had contrived to lose in Brondby after being 1–0 up with two minutes remaining.

HOW THE GROUP STANDS...

TEAMS	P	W	D	L	F	A	Pts
BRONDBY	1	1	0	0	2	1	3
BARCELONA	1	0	1	0	3	3	1
MANCHESTER UNITED	1	0	1	0	3	3	1
BAYERN MUNICH	1	0	0	1	1	2	0

Reds go back to Munich

| GROUP D Game 2 | 30 September 1998 | Olympiastadion | Att: 53,000 | Ref: M Batta (France) | Entertainment: 80% |

Bayern Munich 2 Manchester United 2
United: Scholes, Yorke **Bayern:** Elber, Sheringham (og)

Munich will always figure heavily in United's history. The trip to Bavaria to play German giants Bayern was the first competitive fixture in the city for the club since the tragic Munich air disaster 40 years before, when the plane carrying the Busby Babes crashed after stopping to refuel in Germany on the way back from a European Cup game in Belgrade.

It was a tough assignment for Ferguson and his players as Bayern's general manager, Uli Hoeness, stated that Bayern's team was the best since the club's glory days of the 1970s when, with the likes of Beckenbauer, Moeller and Hoeness in the team, the Germans won the European Cup three times in succession – 1974, '75 and '76. Now coached by Otto Hitzfeld, who masterminded Borussia Dortmund's semi final win over United two years earlier, eight of Bayern's players had just been called up into the German national squad and there were a total of 16 internationals on their books.

United were particularly worried about the height and power of Bayern's big striker Carsten "the Tank" Jancker, who, despite failing a trial at Luton Town four years before, was seen as the major threat to Peter Schmeichel's goal. The Danish keeper was recruited by Ferguson to do some spy work on how to defend against the striker; Schmeichel made a phone call to the coach of Danish club Brondby, who had beaten Bayern in the previous Champions' League meeting.

That defeat was the only hiccup in Bayern's season so far. Playing a 3-5-2 system, they started with six straight wins in the Bundesliga, although in midweek the giants had nearly been humbled in the German Cup by a team of third-division minnows, eventually going through on penalties. They would face United at full strength apart from the injured Thomas Helmer and the flu-ridden Mario Basler. United, for their part, were missing Ryan Giggs (who injured his foot in the side's 2–0 win over Liverpool), Ronny Johnsen and Nicky Butt, suspended after his handball against Barcelona.

United landed in Munich with the Oktoberfest beer festival celebrations (all steins, bratwurst and lederhosen) in full swing, having run a gauntlet of abusive Leeds fans at Manchester airport. The thugs, who were on their way to a UEFA Cup match in Madeira,

Von luvvies
Bayern are nicknamed 'FC Hollywood' by rival fans because the club's highly paid stars are always in the papers bitching about each other.

Late developers
Now Germany's most successful side, Bayern didn't join the Bundesliga until 1969.

Munich minute. The crowd is silent in memory of the 1958 air crash

Where on Earth?

The industrial capital of Bavaria, Munich (population 1.2 million) was the venue for the 1972 Olympics. Heavily bombed during the second world war, it is a modern city most famous for its beer festival.

Wir gedenken der Opfer des Flugzeugunglücks von Manchester United vor 40 Jahren in München

30. SEP. 1998

Skipper Roy Keane leads out United to face old rivals Bayern in an emotion-filled encounter

BAYERN MUNICH — 2

HOME TEAM	GOALS mins	ASSISTS mins	SHOTS ON	SHOTS OFF	SUB'D mins
1 OLIVER KAHN					
2 MARKUS BABBEL					
3 BIXENTE LIZARAZU				1	
8 THOMAS STRUNZ			1	1	
9 GIOVANE ELBER	11				
10 LOTHAR MATTHAUS			1	2	
11 STEFAN EFFENBERG			2	1	
16 JENS JEREMIES			1		82
19 CARSTEN JANCKER		11	1		62
20 HASAN SALIHAMIDZIC			1	4	62
25 THOMAS LINKE			1		

SUBSTITUTES	GOALS mins	ASSISTS mins	SHOTS ON	SHOTS OFF	SUB'D for
4 SAMUEL KUFFOUR					
12 SVEN SCHUER					
17 THORSTEN FINK					#16
18 MICHAEL TARNAT					
24 ALI DAEL			1		#19
28 THORSTEN GOKTAN			1	1	#20

MATCH STATS
SHOTS ON TARGET 7   FOULS 20   OFFSIDES 1
SHOTS OFF TARGET 12   FREE KICKS 17   CORNER KICKS 9

BAYERN'S RATING 68%

MANCHESTER UNITED — 2

AWAY TEAM	GOALS mins	ASSISTS mins	SHOTS ON	OFF	SUB'D mins
1 PETER SCHMEICHEL					
2 GARY NEVILLE					
3 DENIS IRWIN					
6 JAAP STAM					
7 DAVID BECKHAM		29		2	
10 TEDDY SHERINGHAM	90 (og)		1	2	
12 PHIL NEVILLE					
15 JESPER BLOMQVIST					68
16 ROY KEANE				1	
18 PAUL SCHOLES	49		1	1	
19 DWIGHT YORKE	29	49	3	1	

SUBSTITUTES	GOALS mins	ASSISTS mins	SHOTS ON	OFF	SUB'D for
4 DAVID MAY					
9 ANDREW COLE					
14 JORDI CRUYFF					#15
17 RAI VAN DER GOUW					
20 OLE GUNNAR SOLSKJAER					
24 WES BROWN					

MATCH STATS
SHOTS ON TARGET 5   FOULS 17   OFFSIDES 8
SHOTS OFF TARGET 7   FREE KICKS 20   CORNER KICKS 7

UNITED'S RATING 78%

chanted slogans reminding the players about the Munich air disaster. Ferguson and his men, to their credit, did not react, relying on the police to deal with the problem. They had far more worrying things on their mind. A defeat in Munich would be disastrous to their hopes of qualifying from the group.

Fifty-five thousand fans, including an estimated 2,400 from Manchester, packed the Germans' famous Olympic Stadium and let out a huge roar of anticipation after a minute of silence in memory of the United players killed in the '58 disaster. The only person to break the silence was a lone bugler who played out the *Last Post*.

Ten minutes later, the United section of the crowd were furious and the German fans in raptures when Bayern opened the scoring with a goal of technical brilliance involving an interpassing movement between four players. Effenberg delivered a magnificent cross-field pass to find the Brazilian striker Giovane Elber on the left. Elber, holding off big Jaap Stam, crossed the ball through Phil

Neville's legs to an offside-looking Jancker, who played a quick one-two with the Bosnian international Salihamidzic. Jancker in turn played the ball to the feet of Elber, who had continued his run, and, with United's players appealing for offside a second time, the Brazilian curled the ball past Schmeichel. 1–0 against a team which wasn't going to relinquish its lead without one hell of a fight.

United, to their great credit, made the Germans scrap for every ball in the remainder of the match. And just three minutes later they threatened to level the score. Beckham chipped a free kick into the mixer, Stam somehow fashioned a flick-on and Teddy Sheringham, starting just his second game of the season, scuffed his header across the goal but wide of the post. Sheringham, who was in the team to add much-needed height to United's front line,

Joy for Dwight Yorke with his first goal in European competition. Teddy Sheringham applies the congratulations

Bayern's Jancker tries to out-Stam Stam

went close again in the 23rd minute, with a trademark move any *Match Of The Day* viewer would recognise – a volley straight from a Beckham corner which surprised but didn't beat the German keeper, Oliver Kahn.

Beckham then went close with a speciality 30-yard free kick which fizzed wide of the post, and from another free kick found Yorke, who in turn headed wide. Before long United's pressure paid off. Beckham and Sheringham were again involved in a build-up which led to Dwight Yorke scoring his first European goal for United on 29 minutes. Beckham intercepted a ball from the slow-looking Matthaus, then played a slick one-two with Sheringham which gave him room to play in a cross, although this

time he looked half-a-yard offside. As usual, it was a centre of excellence from the blond midfielder, and Yorke's flying far-post header hit the ground before clearing keeper Kahn and bulging the net. It was United's 150th goal in the European Cup. Fittingly, the very first was scored by Munich '58 victim Tommy Taylor back in 1956.

United finished the half on the attack, but were lucky to end it with 11 men on the field. To the tabloid hacks' delight it was David Beckham who should have been sent off. Beckham, already carrying a yellow card from the qualifier, knew a second would put him out of the next game. A shuddering tackle on Effenberg saw the referee get his

Handled

As the match was during the famous Oktoberfest beer festival, some feared United's fans would go on the rampage. But there were just 12 arrests and police praised fans for their peaceful behaviour.

Paul Scholes, he scores goals

book out. Within a minute Beckham could well have seen red after a scuffle with Salihamidzic. With the Bosnian tugging at his shirt Beckham tried to ankle tap him, then swung an elbow into his opponent's chest. French referee Batta, who had officiated England's World Cup match against Romania, chose to ignore the incident, much as he had chosen to ignore the earlier offsides.

United demonstrated their desire to take all three points home and virtually put Bayern out of the competition by continuing to take the game to the Germans after the break, and within three minutes they were ahead – thanks to the skill and perseverance of Paul Scholes. United's carrot-topped midfielder received the ball from Yorke at the edge of the German box after Phil Neville had found the Tobagan from a free kick. With a deftly disguised handball he went past Matthaus (who, looking every minute of his 37 years, could only manage to kick the ball back

in his path when given the chance to clear), and Marcus Babbel, once a Ferguson transfer target. It looked as though Scholes had overrun the ball at that stage, but inexplicably Oliver Kahn dived in without getting the ball and Scholes was left merely needing to pass into an empty goal. 2–1.

It was time for the Germans to pick up the

> 66 **I was satisfied with the performance, but we thought we'd got a good victory. It was one of those things that just kick you in the teeth"** 99
>
> ALEX FERGUSON

pace, but until the last minute they were thwarted by brave saves from Peter Schmeichel who looked like finishing the evening as United's hero, particularly with a fine stop from the effervescent Jeremies. Instead he ended up the villain of the piece after a completely uncharacteristic error allowed Bayern a share of the spoils and left

Ted's down. Sheringham can't believe the events of the last minute of the match.

Right: Peter's bad Herr day

HOW THE GROUP STANDS...

TEAMS	P	W	D	L	F	A	Pts
BARCELONA	2	1	1	0	5	3	4
BRONDBY	2	1	0	1	2	3	3
MANCHESTER UNITED	2	0	2	0	5	5	2
BAYERN MUNICH	2	0	1	1	3	4	1

United with just two points, instead of four, from their opening two fixtures.

The trouble started when Bayern won a throw-in on the left. Their French international wing back Bixente Lizarazu hurled the ball into a crowded penalty area and Schmeichel decided to make the ball his. He leapt over Stam and Neville, both of whom were better placed to clear the danger, in order to punch the ball to safety. However he was left punching thin air, having misjudged the ball's flight completely, and was left watching it sail over his head. On the far post Brazilian striker Giovane Elber and Teddy Sheringham challenged for the cross – it's debatable who got the final touch, but the ball finished the right side of the side-netting and Bayern had salvaged a valuable point.

The drama wasn't yet over. In the depths of injury time Jordi Cruyff acrobatically set up a close-range header for Sheringham, who shot towards the target with some power. But Kahn made a save as valuable as Schmeichel's blunder had been costly and the referee blew his whistle and noted a draw in his book.

United could be excused wanting to go straight home after such a dramatic and suicidal ending to the game, having come so close to winning for the first time away to one of Europe's elite. They would have been the first team ever to beat Bayern at home during the Oktoberfest. But a local no-night-flight ruling meant that their Monarch 757 plane was cancelled and, with the city full of revellers, accommodation wasn't found until one o'clock in the morning. It was a miserable ending to what had seemed destined to be a glorious night.

THE GROUP OF

51

Six of the best

GROUP D | **Game 3** | **21 October 1998** | **Parken Stadium** | **Att: 40,315** | **Ref: V M Pereira (Portugal)** | **Entertainment: 90%**

Brondby 2 Manchester United 6 — United: Giggs 2, Cole, Keane, Yorke, Solskjaer **Brondby:** Daugaard, Sand

"Nice weather for ducks, eh gaffer?"

United's trip to Brondby for their third game in the Champions' League was their second of the season – in the summer they had travelled to Copenhagen to play Schmeichel's old team in a pre-season friendly, and won 6–0. "That was then, this is now," said the Danes, pointing out that their players had had four games that week and were dog-tired. They could also point to a string of successes in Europe over the likes of Tenerife, Karlsruhe and, wait for it, Liverpool – at Anfield.

For United, after two draws in Champions' League matches which they had led for long periods, a win was vital. In fact, in a fortnight in which they were to play Brondby twice, a double over the Danes looked an absolute necessity. "We must win both games," said Fergie, before the first. "If we fail then we don't deserve to be in the quarter-finals anyway."

Peter Schmeichel, who United had bought from Brondby back in 1992, was of course the man of the moment, despite the glaring error in his last Champions' League game against Bayern Munich. Schmeichel, who hadn't played a game

COPENHAGEN

DENMARK

Where on Earth?

Brondby is a suburb of the Danish capital of Copenhagen, a sea port and commercial city (population 1.3 million). Apart from Peter Schmeichel, it is best known for its beer and Little Mermaid sculpture in the harbour.

since then thanks to a stomach injury, is one of the biggest sporting heroes in the country. "Peter Schmeichel is the best goalkeeper in Denmark ever and I am not sure that in my time I will see anyone better," gushed Brondby coach Ebbe Skovdahl in his pre-match spiel. He should know all about the big keeper – he first signed him for Brondby in 1987.

The man most likely to score against United's keeper, Bent Christansen, who had scored 12 goals in 18 European Cup games, was out long-term with a knee injury and Brondby were also without their skipper John Jensen, who Arsenal fans remember with some fondness. For those who did make the team – including World Cup star Ebbe Sand – an £8,000 win bonus was up for grabs, the total Brondby's players received after their shock 2–1 win over Bayern Munich.

United were boosted by the return of their keeper, and were also relieved to see Ryan Giggs recovered from the foot injury which had put him out of the previous Champions' League game. Giggs, seen by Ferguson as a vital cog in his European machine, was to play on the right wing to accommodate Blomqvist playing out on the left, with Scholes and Keane in the centre. "We have a few players who can change the course of a game and Ryan is one," stated Ferguson beforehand. "He has turned into a

"I'll let you score the first two, Giggsy, but I'm getting at least one"

"See Ryan, I always keep my promises"

big-game player." But on the injury and suspension list were David Beckham, Nicky Butt, Teddy Sheringham, Denis Irwin, Ronny Johnsen and David May. The defence saw Stam and Gary Neville in the middle, with Phil Neville and Wes Brown, making his European debut, on the flanks, and Yorke and Cole up front.

In order to accommodate the huge number of fans wanting to see the game it was played (on a night of teeming rain) in the 41,000 capacity Parken Stadium in Copenhagen. Due to a lack of interest (or the sort of dosh necessary for a midweek break in Scandinavia), United returned 1,600 of the 3,200 tickets allocated to them, so the team were expecting quite a hostile atmosphere.

The best way to silence a crowd, however, is to score an early goal and go on to dominate the game, and Manchester United did just that. Within two minutes Wes Brown found space on an overlapping run down the right, and hit a looping ball into the box. The keeper Morgens Krogh looked to have it covered, but was unsighted by a dive in front of

Above: Brondby were terrified of Ryan Giggs

Below: Andy Cole's goal was a beauty

him by Kenneth Rasmussen and spilled the ball. Ryan Giggs was on hand to poke it in from close range, a rare goal with his right foot. It was just the start United needed – though they hadn't shown themselves to be very adept at holding leads in the tournament so far.

United started dominating midfield through Keane and Scholes and, though Soren Colding did manage to test Schmeichel with a long shot, the Reds rarely looked under threat, with Cole going close with a cross-shot. Then, on 21 minutes, Jesper Blomqvist, tugging his sleeves over his hands against the cold, burst down the left and flighted in a cross. Ryan Giggs was waiting at the far post, where he out-jumped Brian Jensen to score his second thumping header of the campaign, and his second goal of the game.

The next goal, on the half hour, was all about the blossoming relationship between Dwight Yorke and Andy Cole. Yorke, in the centre circle, received a shoulder-high ball from midfield with his back to goal. With one deft touch he chested the ball down while turning and beat his marker, Brazilian Vragel Da Silva, and with a second he found Cole, who had made a run to the edge of the box. Cole took the ball past a defender before placing it past the keeper. 3–0.

Another Schmeichel mistake allowed the Danes a glimmer of hope before the interval.

> ❝ **What killed Brondby stone dead was the suddenness of those strikes, because we scored early in each half and it is difficult to recover from that** ❞
>
> ALEX FERGUSON

Watch out, there's a Keano about

Heads we win!

> ❝ I have to admit I didn't think we'd get a score like that. We gave the ball away and were careless at times but our finishing was excellent ❞
>
> ALEX FERGUSON

After Thomas Lindrup had been booked for taking a free kick too quickly, his team-mate Kim Daugaard took his time and hit a 25-yarder low to the right of United's wall. Schmeichel looked like he had his near post covered but the ball fizzed off the greasy surface and through his grasp.

However, it was a rare turning of the Red tide and United continued their exhilarating dominance of the Danes in the second half. On 55 minutes Keane picked up a powerful defensive header some way out of the box and started on a determined run. Just managing to keep the ball under control at some speed, he beat a defender before playing a one-two with

Brøndby IF	2
Manchester U.	6

 ## "It was a bit like a tennis match" "

EBBE SKOVDAHL

BRONDBY   2

HOME TEAM	GOALS mins	ASSISTS mins	SHOTS ON	SHOTS OFF	SUB'D mins
1 MORGENS KROGH					
2 OLE BJUR			1		
4 PER NIELSEN					30
6 ALLAN RAVN JENSEN			1	1	
8 KIM DAUGAARD	35		1		
19 KENNETH RASMUSSEN					
12 EBBE SAND	90		1		
13 BO HANSEN					67
14 SOREN COLDING					
16 BRIAN JENSEN			1		26
24 THOMAS LINDRUP			1	1	

SUBSTITUTES	GOALS mins	ASSISTS mins	SHOTS ON	SHOTS OFF	SUB'D for
5 VRAGEL DA SILVA					#16
9 JESPER THYGESEN					
15 RUBEN BAGGER			2		#13
17 SOREN KROGH					
21 MIKKEL JENSEN					#4
22 EMEKA ANDERSEN					
23 MADS OLSEN					

MATCH STATS
SHOTS ON TARGET	6	FOULS	7	OFFSIDES	1
SHOTS OFF TARGET	4	FREE KICKS	6	CORNER KICKS	10

BRONDBY'S RATING 40%

MANCHESTER UNITED   6

AWAY TEAM	GOALS mins	ASSISTS mins	SHOTS ON	SHOTS OFF	SUB'D mins
1 PETER SCHMEICHEL					
2 GARY NEVILLE					
6 JAAP STAM					
12 PHIL NEVILLE		60			
24 WES BROWN					
15 JESPER BLOMQVIST		21	1	1	
16 ROY KEANE	55		2		
18 PAUL SCHOLES			1		
11 RYAN GIGGS	2, 21		2		60
19 DWIGHT YORKE	60	27, 55, 61	1		64
9 ANDREW COLE	27		4		60

SUBSTITUTES	GOALS mins	ASSISTS mins	SHOTS ON	SHOTS OFF	SUB'D for
17 RAI VAN DER GOUW					
14 JORDI CRUYFF					#11
20 OLE GUNNAR SOLSKJAER	61		1		#9
21 HENNING BERG					
23 MICHAEL CLEGG					
29 JOHN CURTIS					
33 MARK WILSON					#19

MATCH STATS
SHOTS ON TARGET	11	FOULS	6	OFFSIDES	3
SHOTS OFF TARGET	2	FREE KICKS	7	CORNER KICKS	4

UNITED'S RATING 80%

Dwight Yorke and calmly and powerfully sidefooting the ball past Krogh off the inside of the post.

Next up was a rare assist from Phil Neville who broke down the left like Brown had on the right in the first half, and pumped a well-hit cross into the box. Yorke was waiting and he gave the keeper no chance with a thumping header. On the hour, the best goal of a good lot made United the biggest scorers ever in an away game in the Champions' League. Keane, on the left side of midfield, spotted Dwight Yorke with his back to goal and curled in a pass. Yorke, receiving the ball at a difficult height, laid the ball off with his knees to Ole Gunnar Solskjaer who had only been on the pitch a minute, replacing Cole. The Norwegian belted a shot through the legs of a defender, and the rout was complete.

United could afford to take their foot off the pedal and with Yorke and Giggs having joined Cole on the bench for the last half hour, Brondby duly scored a consolation goal in the last minute. In a move that seemed to be taking place in slow motion, Bagger hit in a daisy cutter that Schmeichel managed to

parry, diving to his left. Ebbe Sand was at hand to knock in the easiest and most meaningless goal of his career. He didn't even bother to celebrate.

It was a magnificent performance by United, who had turned the corner after a dodgy period in the Premiership and moved from second from bottom to top place in the Champions' League 'group of death', after Bayern Munich had beaten Barcelona 1–0 in Germany. But afterwards Ferguson, doubtless trying to deter any complacency about the forthcoming fixture with the Danes at Old Trafford, was decidedly downbeat. "It was not a great performance. The conditions did not help because the pitch was very heavy but we were still sloppy and careless at times."

HOW THE GROUP STANDS...

TEAMS	P	W	D	L	F	A	Pts
MANCHESTER UNITED	3	1	2	0	11	7	5
BARCELONA	3	1	1	1	5	4	4
BAYERN MUNICH	3	1	1	1	4	4	4
BRONDBY	3	1	0	2	4	9	3

Game, set and match

GROUP D   Game 4   4 November 1998   Old Trafford   Att: 53,250   Ref: M Lubos (Slovakia)   Entertainment: 90%

Manchester United 5 Brondby 0 <small>United: Beckham, Cole, P Neville, Yorke, Scholes</small>

Afortnight after hitting Brondby for six to go to the top of the 'group of death', United faced the Danes again, this time at Old Trafford. Naturally, all the talk before the game was of guarding against complacency. Brondby, after all, had beaten Liverpool 1–0 at Anfield in the UEFA Cup three years previously and, a year before, beaten Karlsruhe 5–0 in the same competition – in Germany. "It's important that we do well if we want to win this section," said Ferguson before the game. "I think they will make it more difficult for us this time."

United's players had obviously got the message as in pre-match press conferences they were echoing the same sentiments. "People are expecting a lot of goals tonight," said Dwight Yorke. "But that is not the number-one target. The priority for us is to win the match and get the three points which will keep us on the top of the group."

"We would accept a 1–0 win," reiterated Phil Neville, "because that is all we need."

Wily Danish coach Ebbe Skovdahl was doing all he could to play down his side's chances at

Yorke: "People are expecting lots of goals tonight"
Below: David Beckham makes it 1–0

Old Trafford, and thus increase the United fans and players' expectations. After two United wins of 6–0 and 6–2 he joked, "I wonder what the score will be in the third set," and added, "United are almost unstoppable at the moment and if we go back to Denmark having lost by only one or two goals, it will feel like a victory." Despite his kidology the chilling fact was that a Brondby victory would see them leapfrog over United, and possibly top the group!

The bad news on the injury front was that Ryan Giggs, who had scored United's first two goals in the first leg, was out of the running with a broken bone in his all-important left foot. The good news was that Jesper Blomqvist had just scored his first goal for the club in Giggs' position in a 4–1 win at Everton and that on the other side of the field a certain David Beckham was back from suspension. The Danes were without the suspended Thomas Lindrup but were pleased that that their skipper, the former Arsenal player John Jensen, was back from a one-match ban himself.

Everything added up to the fact that United desperately needed an early goal to settle any nerves and get into gear. So a Beckham free-kick 30 yards out on six minutes bode well. The Danes formed a three-man wall, and Beckham hit the ball where a fourth should have been. The speed, curl and accuracy of his delivery fooled Brondby's second-string keeper Emeka Anderson, and the ball flew between his outstretched glove and his right-hand post. 1–0, and the floodgates were open.

A couple of minutes later, United nearly sealed the game, with a brilliant team move that epitomised the surging power play which had produced 21 goals in October. Scholes battled to win the ball in midfield, Cole picked it up,

❝ It was the best goal I've ever seen us score at Old Trafford ❞

PETER SCHMEICHEL ON ANDREW COLE'S STRIKE

Cole gets the best goal Schmeichel ever saw United score at Old Trafford

delivered it to Yorke and sprinted goalwards. Yorke spotted Keane on the left and quickly released the ball to him, with Cole jumping over it *en route*. Keane checked the ball with his left foot, beat his man and looped a right-foot cross into the box where Yorke was waiting, semi-marked. A Brondby defender made a desperate lunge for the ball to prevent it reaching its target, but only managed to spoon it over his keeper and onto the post. Both Cole and Yorke were ready for the rebound, and Cole pushed in front to shoot from close range. The shot was blocked, and Brondby breathed again.

B ut not for long. Another brilliant move showed why people were drooling over the attacking partnership of Yorke and Cole. Keane found Blomqvist on the left and the Swede beat a man before laying a diagonal ball into the box towards Cole, who did a dummy, allowing it to run through to Yorke, and carried on his run into the box. First time, Yorke found his strike partner again, and, from a narrow angle, Cole delicately chipped the ball between the keeper and the post, with the

Clockwise: Blomqvist starts to enjoy his United career; Scholes always enjoys scoring and Wes Brown is just happy to be in the team

Brondby defenders left standing to admire the beauty of the act. Later, Peter Schmeichel said it was the best goal he had ever seen United score at Old Trafford. Cole pointed to Yorke's number during the goal celebrations to indicate the credit should go to his strike partner, but in truth he deserved the plaudits himself.

United's superiority was outlined by the fact that the next goal was all Phil Neville. The right back collected the ball in his own half, played a square ball to Beckham, and ran into space. Beckham played the ball straight back to him and he dribbled into central Danish territory. Yorke, as ever, was waiting outside the box –

MANCHESTER UNITED					5
HOME TEAM	GOALS mins	ASSISTS mins	SHOTS ON	OFF	SUB'D mins
1 PETER SCHMEICHEL					
2 GARY NEVILLE					
12 PHIL NEVILLE	16		1		32
6 JAAP STAM				1	
3 DENIS IRWIN					
7 DAVID BECKHAM	7	28, 62	2	4	
16 ROY KEANE					
15 JESPER BLOMQVIST					46
18 PAUL SCHOLES	62		1	1	
19 DWIGHT YORKE	28	13, 16	2	3	
9 ANDREW COLE	13		3		55

SUBSTITUTES	GOALS mins	ASSISTS mins	SHOTS ON	OFF	SUB'D for
17 RAI VAN DER GOUW					
5 RONNY JOHNSEN					
8 NICK BUTT					
14 JORDI CRUYFF			1		#15
20 OLE GUNNAR SOLSKJAER			1		#9
29 JOHN CURTIS					
24 WES BROWN					#12

MATCH STATS
SHOTS ON TARGET 9 FOULS 9 OFFSIDES 1
SHOTS OFF TARGET 11 FREE KICKS 13 CORNER KICKS 7

UNITED'S RATING 80%

BRONDBY					0
AWAY TEAM	GOALS mins	ASSISTS mins	SHOTS ON	OFF	SUB'D mins
22 EMEKA ANDERSEN					
14 SOREN COLDING			1		
4 PER NIELSEN					
19 KENNETH RASMUSSEN					
7 JOHN JENSEN			1		
2 OLE BJUR				1	74
6 ALAN RAVN JENSEN			1		
8 KIM DAUGAARD			3		
15 RUBEN BAGGER			2		68
12 EBBE SAND		1			77
18 AURELIUS SKARBALIJUS			1		

SUBSTITUTES	GOALS mins	ASSISTS mins	SHOTS ON	OFF	SUB'D for
30 KIM DREJS					
3 ANDERS BJERREGAARD					
5 VRAGEL DA SILVA					
9 JESPER THYGESEN			1		#15
13 BO HANSEN			1		#12
17 SOREN KROGH			1		#2
21 MIKKEL JENSEN					

MATCH STATS
SHOTS ON TARGET 1 FOULS 13 OFFSIDES 3
SHOTS OFF TARGET 12 FREE KICKS 9 CORNER KICKS 4

BRONDBY RATING 32%

Neville junior played the ball to him and carried on his run. He received the return pass on the edge of the box, ran between two defenders and thumped it past the keeper for only his second goal for the club.

Before half time United added a fourth, for which most of the credit must go to Jesper Blomqvist. The Swedish winger broke up a Brondby attack in the United penalty box and set off on a run. Two midfielders tried to block his path, but he dribbled through the space between them and started looking round for passing options. (He was still, at this point, in his own half.) None immediately presented itself, so he carried on into Brondby territory before spotting Beckham, who had drifted almost unmarked to the edge of the Brondby box, on the left-hand side. You should know better than to give the England midfielder time for a cross, and you should know better than to only half-mark Dwight Yorke once it's been delivered. The Tobagan headed the ball powerfully past the keeper, and double figures looked to be on the cards.

United, however, took their foot off the pedal in the second half, the highlight of which was an individual goal by Paul Scholes. The ginger midfielder picked up the ball outside the box on the right and shaped to smash in a Bobby Charlton special. The defender in front of him was left trying to block thin air as Scholes pulled out of the shot, shimmied past him and on towards the next defender. With a touch of his right foot he sidestepped past, and with a crack of his left he buried the ball – 5–0.

United hadn't quite managed a tennis score against the Danes, but the rout was complete, and confidence sky high. Bayern's late goal in Barcelona, earning them a 2–1 win, meant a victory in the Nou Camp would virtually qualify Ferguson's men for the quarter-finals. The players and fans couldn't wait for the game.

HOW THE GROUP STANDS...

TEAMS	P	W	D	L	F	A	Pts
MANCHESTER UNITED	4	2	2	0	16	7	8
BAYERN MUNICH	4	2	1	1	6	5	7
BARCELONA	4	1	1	2	6	6	4
BRONDBY	4	1	0	3	4	14	3

Homage to Catalonia

| GROUP D Game 5 | 25 November 1998 | Nou Camp | Att: 67,650 | Ref: G Benko (Austria) | Entertainment: 95% |

Barcelona 3 Manchester United 3 United: Yorke 2, Cole Barcelona: Anderson, Rivaldo 2

Both managers had demons to banish before the penultimate group-stage Champions' League match between Barcelona and Manchester United at the Nou Camp on 25 November. Alex Ferguson's were old ones – memories of the 4–0 mauling that United had suffered at the feet of Romario, Stoichkov and co in the same stadium four years before. United, not used to losing, were absolutely thrashed that night and might well have lost by much more had Barcelona not taken their foot off the throttle. Only three fit players remained from that team, but there wasn't a United player who wasn't aware of the psychological blow that night had dealt to the club. "We were lucky to get nil," remembered Denis Irwin, who lined up in the Nou Camp for the second time, alongside Nick Butt and Roy Keane. When Ferguson was asked what he remembered of that night in a pre-match press conference he was unwilling to divulge. "Nothing" he replied flatly. Like we believed him.

Louis van Gaal's worries were much closer to hand. The press and Catalan public had long ago turned against the Dutchman, despite the previous season's League and Cup double. For one they were suspicious of his policy of filling the team with Dutch compatriots – there were already six and counting at the club. What's more, they were desperately worried that, in proud Barcelona's centenary year, the club wouldn't manage to qualify for the quarter-finals of a competition, the final of which was to be

played at the Nou Camp in May. While United had spent the autumn gorging themselves on goals against Brondby, Barça had contrived to lose home and away against Bayern Munich, detonating their dreams into ruins and building up the German team's out of the rubble.

To make matters worse, Barcelona were facing a personnel crisis that threatened to leave them

Below: the calm before the storm

Neck and neck

Before this fixture United had met Barcelona six times. Their record against the Spanish giants (being led out by Maradona, above) is:

P6 W2 D2 L2 F10 A13

> ❝ I know we can afford to lose, but I don't think losing is ever healthy. Winning is the name of the game ❞
>
> ALEX FERGUSON BEFORE THE GAME

with too few players to man the bench. Patrick Kluivert and Mauricio Pellegrino, of course, were ineligible having signed too late to play in the Champions' League. Also out were Guardiola, Cocu, Luis Enrique and Nadal. United were missing their inspirational winger Ryan Giggs, as well as Johnsen, Sheringham and Cruyff. If they needed any motivation, in a game they didn't have to win, it came from van Gaal. "It may be that Manchester United are the richest club in the world," he growled. "But

Brondby) and they were out. For United, a win would mean that they only needed to draw at home to Bayern in their last match, whereas a defeat would mean that they would almost certainly have to beat the Germans. In the grand scheme of things, a draw wasn't significantly different to a defeat. Because of the lack of the sort of must-win urgency that usually surrounds such matches, Ferguson fired an anti-complacency broadside at his men. "I know we can afford to lose, but I don't think losing is

United enjoyed the Nou Camp so much they decided to return in May

> ❝ People will say that coming here and getting a draw is a great result, but we don't think so. There is more disappointment than satisfaction because we were ahead twice against Barcelona and in Munich, and we let go of our advantage ❞
>
> JAAP STAM

win the Champions' League? I don't think so. Money does not determine this, the qualities of the players determine this, and the qualities of the technical staff." A further fillip to Ferguson and his players arrived in a car from Toulouse before the game – and Fergie invited Eric Cantona to sit with the players in the dressing room before the match, an offer he politely refused.

All week, fans in Barcelona and Manchester had been arguing about what their teams needed to do to stand a chance of qualifying. For Barcelona it was easy – anything but victory (assuming Bayern would beat faltering

ever healthy. Winning is the name of the game."

None of the 67,650 fans in the stadium (such is the fickleness of the Catalans it was almost half empty!) or the millions watching at home and in the pubs could expect to be served up a match as exciting or full of attacking football as the first group game between the clubs two months earlier, which finished 3–3. But any mad optimists who had were rewarded with a game that, if anything, turned out to be even better.

Barcelona demonstrated that rumours of their decline were greatly exaggerated by scoring on their first attack in the first minute of the game. After winning a throw on the left, Sergi and

The mighty Johan

Jordi Cruyff's dad, the legendary Johan, was Barcelona's manager when they won their first and only European Cup in 1992.

"I just ran to the corner to celebrate. I had no idea a bunch of United fans were in there among the Barcelona supporters" ANDY COLE

Introducing the best attack in Europe. Starring Andy Cole. . .

. . . and Dwight Yorke

"Anything you can do. . ."

66 "In the end it was our attacking play that kept us in the game after a terrible start" 99

ALEX FERGUSON

Rivaldo fashioned a neat passage of interplay to serve the ball to Giovanni wide on the left, halfway into United's half. He angled a cross into the box towards Figo which was weakly headed away by Irwin to the feet of Sonny Anderson, just outside the box. The Brazilian, who could have scored a hat-trick at Old Trafford, turned past a stumbling Gary Neville, found space in the box and crashed the ball past the diving Schmeichel. Thousands of Catalans watching at home suddenly wished they'd got off their arses and gone to the game.

The Catalans had started the match, if anything, more exuberantly than United had started against them at Old Trafford, and Ferguson's men looked like they were playing a different ball game – one that involved not having to touch it. Chance after chance was made by the Spanish forwards (or Brazilian, to be more exact), the best falling to Anderson who sliced through the United defence onto a perfect through ball by Rivaldo, only to have his shot blocked by the looming Schmeichel. On another occasion, with the United defenders oddly backing off, Rivaldo cracked a 25-yarder that Schmeichel tipped round the post. Then, on 24 minutes, Blomqvist, whose defensive qualities are often underestimated, robbed Okunowo wide on the left inside his own half and charged upfield. He

Now you know...
Barcelona's museum at the Nou Camp
stadium receives 650,000 visitors a year

Who's smiling now?

Yorke-power

only had one positive passing option – the sprinting Dwight Yorke, ahead of him to his right. He found him with a perfect through ball aimed at a gap between two Barcelona defenders. Yorke, with the ball at his feet in the box, had time to pick his spot despite the speed he was moving at, and hit the space between the keeper and his right-hand post with wicked accuracy. They might not have deserved it but, incredibly, United were level.

Barcelona, mightily miffed, turned on the pressure again, and United had Schmeichel to thank for taking them to the interval on level terms. A Celares cross from the right on the half hour missed two men, but was picked up by Figo on the right-hand edge of the box. Figo's turn completely flummoxed Beckham and he found the space to slam in a shot. Schmeichel could only parry, diving to his right, and was alarmed to see Zender and Anderson running in on the rebound. Not for long though, because a split second later, dropping groundwards at the end of his dive, he managed to get a second touch on the ball which carried it to safety.

United started the second half with renewed conviction and were rewarded for their efforts with a goal which will be replayed for years to show the brilliant quasi-telepathic relationship between Dwight Yorke and Andy Cole. Keane started the move from the right wing, passing a diagonal ball forward to Yorke who was running towards Barça's box. Yorke, aware that Cole was running behind him, stepped over the ball, taking out a defender in the process, and carried on his run. Cole tapped the ball first time into Yorke's path and continued with his

❝ **When you score three goals you have to be pleased. In a game of this nature we have to be satisfied with a draw because of the way both sides were attacking** ❞

ALEX FERGUSON

“ **You've got to admire Rivaldo. He was their star player and the man who made all the difference for Barcelona** ” ALEX FERGUSON

own run. With the Spanish defenders in complete disarray, Yorke returned the compliment with another first-time ball to his partner, now on the edge of the box. Cole controlled the ball with his first touch and carefully placed it past Hesp into the net with his second. It was a goal worthy of winning a European Cup Final, let alone taking the lead in a group match, and the gleeful celebrations of the two players involved wouldn't have been out of place in that setting.

Barcelona, however, weren't finished off by the move, and within three minutes again proved that they are most effective when the chips are down. They won a free kick about 35 yards out, well outside the box. Rivaldo stepped over the ball with resolve and curled in a shot that so bamboozled Schmeichel that the ITV commentator thought there had been a deflection. There was no such thing, just an enormous amount of curl on the ball that saw it bounce before creeping inside the post. The big Dane had not even moved.

BARCELONA — 3

HOME TEAM	GOALS mins	ASSISTS mins	SHOTS ON	SHOTS OFF	SUB'D mins
13 RUUD HESP					
22 GBENGA OKUNOWO				1	
12 SERGI BARJUAN		73			
2 MICHAEL REIZIGER					
8 ALBERT CELADES LOPEZ				1	
26 XAVI HERNANDEZ CRUZ				3	
23 BOLO ZENDEN					
7 LUIS FIGO				1	
11 RIVALDO	57, 73		6	2	
10 GIOVANNI DE OLIVERA			1	2	
9 SONNY ANDERSON	1		2		

SUBSTITUTES	GOALS mins	ASSISTS mins	SHOTS ON	SHOTS OFF	SUB'D for
25 FRANCESCO ARNAU					
16 DRAGAN CIRIC					
24 ROGER GARCIA					
27 MARIO ROSAS MONTERO					
33 IBAN ALONSO CUADRADO					

MATCH STATS
SHOTS ON TARGET 10 FOULS 7 OFFSIDES 3
SHOTS OFF TARGET 9 FREE KICKS 20 CORNER KICKS 15

BARÇA'S RATING 85%

MANCHESTER UNITED — 3

AWAY TEAM	GOALS mins	ASSISTS mins	SHOTS ON	SHOTS OFF	SUB'D mins
1 PETER SCHMEICHEL					
24 WES BROWN			1		
3 DENIS IRWIN					
6 JAAP STAM					
2 GARY NEVILLE					
16 ROY KEANE				2	
18 PAUL SCHOLES				2	
7 DAVID BECKHAM		68			81
15 JESPER BLOMQVIST		25			
19 DWIGHT YORKE	25, 68	53	3	2	
9 ANDREW COLE	53		2	2	

SUBSTITUTES	GOALS mins	ASSISTS mins	SHOTS ON	SHOTS OFF	SUB'D for
17 RAI VAN DER GOUW					
12 PHIL NEVILLE					
8 NICKY BUTT			1		#7
20 OLE GUNNAR SOLSKJAER					
21 HENNING BERG					
29 JOHN CURTIS					
33 MARK WILSON					

MATCH STATS
SHOTS ON TARGET 6 FOULS 20 OFFSIDES 7
SHOTS OFF TARGET 7 FREE KICKS 7 CORNER KICKS 6

UNITED'S RATING 80%

Força Barça
Despite having won the European Cup only once, Barcelona are the second most successful club in all European competitions. In total, they have won eight trophies – the European Cup (1992), four Cup-Winners' Cups, including the above Gary Lineker-inspired one (1979, '82, '89, '97), and three Fairs Cups (it later became the UEFA, 1958, '60, '66). The most successful side of all are Barça's arch rivals Real Madrid with nine.

Beckham in Barça

ANDERSON
RIVALDO (2)
BARCELONA 3
MANCHESTER UNITED 3
YORKE (2)
COLE

For once he didn't shout at his defenders, instead he booted the ball into the net again, before thumping it back upfield.

It was United's turn to grab the initiative and Beckham, perhaps miffed that Rivaldo had scored a free-kick as good as one of his own, started down the right on 67 minutes. After a neat bit of Yorke-and-Cole interplay the latter found Beckham on the wing with enough room to hit in a cross. Yorke had continued his run into the box and, though the ball bounced before it reached him, he directed a diving header towards the goal. It flashed past the post, skimming the side netting. But the move turned out to be a dress rehearsal, as shortly after, an identical cross reached the diving Yorke without bouncing and the Tobagan powered the ball past Hesp and into the goal. 3–2 to United.

At that point, with both sides showing brilliance in attack and fragility in defence, few would have betted against further goals and it was Barcelona, fighting for their lives in the competition, who took control of the final stages of the match. With 14 minutes left on the clock,

wing back Sergi, seeing Rivaldo in the box, sent in a looping cross towards him, even though he was double marked by Neville and Stam. This didn't bother the Brazilian, who controlled the ball on his chest, and scissor-kicked it past Schmeichel in exactly the same spot he had beaten the Dane 20 minutes before. Remarkably, once again, the score was 3–3, with 15 minutes left to play.

Rivaldo hadn't finished his one-man show. Just minutes after his second goal, at least 35 yards out, he hit a crashing drive that smashed against the crossbar, with or without the help of a Schmeichel fingertip. Then, with seconds remaining, he received a pass on the edge of the box from Giovanni, delivered a back-

"Can I borrow Yorke, Mr Ferguson?"

heeled one-two return to his team-mate, to put him through the defence and one on one with the keeper. Not many keepers would have had the speed of thought and action of the Dane, who made himself big to block the shot. Barcelona were out of the tournament. With Bayern beating Brondby 2–0, United needed a win in their last match over the Germans to definitely qualify, though one suspected a draw would do the trick. . .

BARCELONA

Where on Earth?

A bustling port with a Mediterranean climate, Barcelona is Spain's second largest city (population two million) and the capital of the fiercely proud region of Catalonia. It is famous for its architecture as well as its football team.

HOW THE GROUP STANDS...

TEAMS	P	W	D	L	F	A	Pts
BAYERN MUNICH	5	3	1	1	8	5	10
MANCHESTER UNITED	5	2	3	0	19	10	9
BARCELONA	5	1	2	2	9	9	5
BRONDBY	5	1	0	4	4	16	3

Bayern time

GROUP D Game 6 | 9 December 1998 | Old Trafford | Att: 54,434 | Ref: D Jol (Holland) | Entertainment: 80%

Manchester United 1 Bayern Munich 1 United: Keane Bayern: Salihamidzic

Nobody really seemed sure of what result United had to achieve before their final Group D game against Bayern Munich at Old Trafford. Indeed, the permutations were complicated. Out of the six groups, the six winners automatically qualified, while the two runners-up went through by dint of points won, then goal difference, then goals scored. A United win would qualify them as group winners, while a draw would only suffice if other results went their way. Even a defeat, on a lucky night, might be enough.

Alex Ferguson, as confused as the rest of us (United don't have a mathematician on their books for such situations) made one thing clear – he would go for a win against the German team, as he had done in October. The Germans, remember, had luckily snatched a last-gasp equaliser in the Munich game after an uncharacteristic mistake from Peter Schmeichel. "People have been trying to work out all the variations," he mused, "but if we win, we're through. That's what we're aiming for."

Surprisingly, this was to be Bayern's first-ever visit to Old Trafford, but manager Otto Hitzfeld was no stranger to the Theatre of Dreams – he had turned it into a field of nightmares with his previous team, Borussia Dortmund, in the semi-final two years earlier, when United, looking to overcome a 1–0 defeat in Dortmund, went a goal down after six minutes and couldn't find a reply; Dortmund went on to win the Final against Juventus.

Before the United-Bayern game Hitzfeld blamed United's defeat against Dortmund on

On a wing. . .

. . . and a prayer

Ferguson's fierce desire to win the European Cup. "I know it is something that burns inside him still," he said. "In any game like that it is a question of the nerve of the players. For whatever reason, maybe because Ferguson wanted it too much and expressed that feeling, his side were too inhibited."

But the comments (interpreted by the dear old *Daily Mail* as 'Fergie Gives his Players the Jitters says Bayern Boss'), didn't start a war of words between the managers, with Hitzfeld going on to praise his foes-to-be. "Manchester United have one of the best football teams English football has seen," he cooed. "They play a very modern game, very European with a high technical level. What Alex Ferguson has done has been sensational." Ferguson didn't

❝ Manchester United have one of the best football teams English football has seen. They play a very modern game, very European with a high technical level. What Alex Ferguson has done has been sensational ❞ BAYERN BOSS OTTO HITZFELD

The food of dreams

The wrath of Kahn

Germany v England

Bayern Munich had played two other English clubs in a European Cup Final. In 1975, they beat Leeds United 2–0 for the second of their three-in-a-row triumphs (with the mighty Sepp Maier, above, in goal), but in 1982 they lost to eventual champions, Aston Villa.

seem to be too worried about the prospect of a third defeat at the hands of the Germans. "I don't think they'll be killing themselves to beat us," he said. "A draw will suit them and they'll probably defend deep." Hitzfeld carried on the friendly fire with a nice thought: "I hope we both qualify for the quarter-finals."

Ferguson was boosted by the rare luxury of a full squad to pick from with Ryan Giggs having recovered from his foot injury. Bayern were without Mehmet Scholl and Iranian striker Ali Daei, and had nine players one yellow card away from a suspension, but their top 20 players were given a boost when they learnt that they were on a £100,000-a-man bonus if they got through to the quarter-finals.

Maybe it was the incentive of the money, maybe it was simply their habitual ruthless efficiency, but from the start the Germans took the game to United. Their close, efficient passing meant that the Reds only threatened on the counter-attack. However when they did fight back, they did so well, and created a series of chances in a cut-and-thrust first half.

United went close first, with a beautifully weighted cross-field Beckham pass finding Giggs on the left wing. Giggs laid the ball into the box to Cole, whose quick shot on the turn was blocked, only to fall to Yorke, who fired hastily over the bar. Then Keane found Giggs, with his back to goal in the penalty 'D'. Giggs' clever flick found Cole whose shot-on-the-turn just flashed wide.

On 16 minutes, it was Bayern's turn to go close when Bosnian international Salihamidzic

ran onto an Effenberg pass and crossed low into the box. Brazilian Giovane Elber nipped in front of a slow-looking Gary Neville and hit in a shot, which finished just wide of its mark. Then on 29 minutes Stefan Effenberg hit a deadly Beckham-like free kick into the box. Alex Zickler met it neatly with his head and beat Pete Schmeichel, but not Roy Keane, who somehow managed to hook it off the goal-line.

There were further chances at either end before the deadlock was broken by United. Stam's defensive header found Beckham on the right wing. A beautiful diagonal pass into the box just eluded Giggs, but the Welshman was quick enough to retrieve the ball on the left, beat the leaden-footed Strunz near the byline and deliver a well-weighted ball back to Keane, who'd made an untracked run to the edge of the box. Keane thumped a daisy-cutter to the goalkeeper's right. 1–0.

Ronny Johnsen appeared out of the dressing room in the second half, replacing the injured Irwin, and nearly wrapped it up for United in their first attack. A Beckham corner was flicked across the goal by Keane, but Johnsen hit thin air with his volley and, when the ball rebounded back towards him, blasted it over the top.

It was a brace of errors that United were to rue as Bayern regained the momentum they had lost after United's goal. On 47 minutes Samuel Kuffour hit in a shot which was saved by Schmeichel, to the relief of United's players and fans. The relief, however, was short-lived. Ten minutes later an Effenberg corner was headed down to the edge of the six-yard box

Keane as Colman's

Runners-up League

They may call it the Champions' League, but the two qualifiers – and eventual finalists – from Group D had both finished runners-up in their respective league campaigns and had had to qualify for the group stages. Meanwhile, Arsenal boss, Arsène Wenger, above, predicted that one of the sides in this group would go on to win the European Cup in May.

HOW THE GROUP FINISHED...

TEAMS	P	W	D	L	F	A	Pts
BAYERN MUNICH	6	3	2	1	9	6	11
MANCHESTER UNITED	6	2	4	0	20	11	10
BARCELONA	6	2	2	2	11	9	8
BRONDBY	6	1	0	5	4	18	3

by Strunz. With Schmeichel stranded, lying on his back, Bayern were quicker to react and if Salihamidzic hadn't poked it into the net, Elber surely would have. 1–1.

Chances were created at both ends as each side tried to make sure of automatic qualification. Giggs, Elber and Scholes missed when they might have scored, and Cole flicked a neat Beckham cross wide. Then, with 15 minutes still on the clock, it was all over. To United fans' frustration, their team either played keep-ball or allowed the Germans to do the same.

The United faithful weren't to know it at the time, but other results, largely a 2–0 Juventus victory over Rosenborg, had gone their way, and Otto Hitzfeld had let Ferguson know this. Ferguson had translated the information to his players and both teams had ceased hostilities. So while the players finished the game in the calm certainty that both sides were safely through, most of the fans were in the dark and not shy of letting their frustrations be heard.

After the final whistle Hitzfeld and Ferguson chatted amicably on their way to the dressing room after a non-aggression pact Stalin and Hitler would have been proud of. Like the two second world war leaders, however, the peace was to prove merely temporary.

MANCHESTER UNITED — 1

HOME TEAM	GOALS mins	ASSISTS mins	SHOTS ON	SHOTS OFF	SUB'D mins
1 PETER SCHMEICHEL					
24 WES BROWN					
6 JAAP STAM		1			
2 GARY NEVILLE					
3 DENIS IRWIN					45
7 DAVID BECKHAM		1			
16 ROY KEANE	43	1			
18 PAUL SCHOLES			2		
10 TEDDY SHERINGHAM		1	2		
12 RYAN GIGGS		43	2		
9 ANDREW COLE		1	3		
19 DWIGHT YORKE		1	2		63

SUBSTITUTES	GOALS mins	ASSISTS mins	SHOTS ON	SHOTS OFF	SUB'D for
17 RAI VAN DER GOUW					
5 RONNY JOHNSEN			1		#3
8 NICKY BUTT					#19
10 TEDDY SHERINGHAM					
12 PHIL NEVILLE					

MATCH STATS
SHOTS ON TARGET 5	FOULS 16	OFFSIDES 4	UNITED'S RATING 68%
SHOTS OFF TARGET 10	FREE KICKS 21	CORNER KICKS 10	

BAYERN MUNICH — 1

AWAY TEAM	GOALS mins	ASSISTS mins	SHOTS ON	SHOTS OFF	SUB'D mins
1 OLIVER KAHN					
10 LOTHAR MATTHAUS			1		61
2 MARKUS BABBEL			1		
4 SAMUEL KUFFOUR			1		
8 THOMAS STRUNZ		56	1	1	
16 JENS JEREMIES			1		
11 STEFAN EFFENBERG			1	1	
20 HASAN SALIHAMIDZIC	57		1		
3 BIXENTE LIZARAZU			1		
9 GIOVANE ELBER			2		81
21 ALEXANDER ZICKLER			1		81

SUBSTITUTES	GOALS mins	ASSISTS mins	SHOTS ON	SHOTS OFF	SUB'D for
12 SVEN SCHUER					
25 THOMAS LINKE					#10
5 THOMAS HELMER					
14 MARIO BASLER					#21
18 MICHAEL TARNAT					
19 CARSTEN JANCKER					9

MATCH STATS
SHOTS ON TARGET 3	FOULS 21	OFFSIDES 2	BAYERN'S RATING 78%
SHOTS OFF TARGET 8	FREE KICKS 16	CORNER KICKS 6	

The group of death
Finally, two are killed off

16 September 1998

Brondby 2
Bayern Munich 1

0–1 (Babbel 76)
1–1 (Helmer 87 og)
2–1 (Ravn 93)

Manchester United 3
Barcelona 3

1–0 (Giggs 17)
2–0 (Scholes 24)
2–1 (Anderson 47)
2–2 (Giovanni 60 pen)
3–2 (Beckham 64)
3–3 (Luis Enrique 71 pen)
(Butt, United, sent off 70)

30 September 1998

Barcelona 2
Brondby 0

1–0 (Anderson 44)
2–0 (Anderson 85)

Bayern Munich 2
Manchester United 2

1–0 (Elber 11)
1–1 (Yorke 29)
2–1 (Scholes 49)
2–2 (Sheringham 90 og)

21 October 1998

Bayern Munich 1
Barcelona 0

1–0 (Effenberg 45)

Brondby 2
Manchester United 6

1–0 (Giggs 2)
2–0 (Giggs 21)
3–0 (Cole 27)
3–1 (Daugaard 35)
4–1 (Keane 55)
5–1 (Yorke 60)
6–1 (Solskjaer 61)
6–2 (Sand 90)

4 November 1998

Barcelona 1
Bayern Munich 2

1–0 (Giovanni 29 pen)
1–1 (Zickler 48)
1–2 (Salihamidzic 87)

Manchester United 5
Brondby 0

1–0 (Beckham 7)
2–0 (Cole 13)
3–0 (P Neville 16)
4–0 (Yorke 28)
5–0 (Scholes 62)

25 November 1998

Bayern Munich 2
Brondby 0

1–0 (Jancker 51)
2–0 (Basler 57)

Barcelona 3
Manchester United 3

1–0 (Anderson 1)
1–1 (Yorke 25)
2–1 (Rivaldo 57)
2–2 (Cole 53)
2–3 (Yorke 68)
3–3 (Rivaldo 73)

9 December 1998

Brondby 0
Barcelona 2

0–1 (Figo 6)
0–2 (Ferreira 36)

Manchester United 1
Bayern Munich 1

1–0 (Keane 42)
1–1 (Salihamidzic 56)

Flying Rivaldo

The Group of Death really lived up to its name but the first two places were effectively settled in the third and fourth matches, both of them double headers. United, in brilliant attacking form, smashed Brondby 6–2 and 5–0 and Bayern did the double over Barcelona, winning 1–0 at home and coming back from being a goal down to beat the Spanish Champions 2–1 at the Nou Camp.

Barcelona, despite holding United twice to 3–3 draws, were the disappointment in a group many expected them to win. In Rivaldo (left), the scorer of three goals and creator of many others, however, they had one of the stars of the group. Top scorer was Dwight Yorke (below) with five goals in his first season in the Champions' League and Manchester United finished top scorers of all the teams in the group stages, with a magnificent 20 goals – though they did let in 11.

FINAL GROUP D TABLE

TEAMS	P	W	D	L	F	A	Pts
BAYERN MUNICH	6	3	2	1	9	6	11
MANCHESTER UNITED	6	2	4	0	20	11	10
BARCELONA	6	2	2	2	11	9	8
BRONDBY	6	1	0	5	4	18	3

Champions undone

Arsenal falter as Kiev rocket through

Rebrov sneaks past the Arsenal back four

Arsenal looked home and dry in this group before their double header with Dynamo Kiev, who they could have virtually knocked out by beating them at home – Wembley rather than Highbury – as early as the third game. Instead Rebrov equalised in the last minute, Arsenal were smashed 3–1 in the Ukraine and Kiev went on to win the group with some comfort, their strike force of Shevchenko and Rebrov looking like the best pairing in the continent (bar maybe Yorke and Cole).

Arsenal had only themselves to blame as they made a habit of letting in late goals (a similar last-gasp equaliser stopped them from winning their opening game in Lens) and only a win by their reserve team away in Greece stopped them from finishing last.

16 September 1998

Lens 1
Arsenal..1

0–1 (Overmars 51)
1–1 (Vairelles 90)

Panathinaikos...................................2
Dynamo Kiev....................................1

0–1 (Rebrov 31)
1–1 (Mykland 56)
2–1 (Liberopoulos 69)

30 September 1998

Dynamo Kiev....................................1
Lens 1

1–0 (Shevchenko 61)
1–1 (Vairelles 62)

Arsenal 2
Panathinaikos...................................1

1–0 (Adams 62)
2–0 (Keown 75)
2–1(Pereira Da Silva 87)

21 October 1998

Arsenal..1
Dynamo Kiev....................................1

1–0 (Bergkamp 74)
1–1 (Rebrov 90)

Lens 1
Panathinaikos...................................0

1–0 (Eloi 80)

4 November 1998

Dynamo Kiev....................................3
Arsenal..1

1–0 (Rebrov 11 pen)
2–0 (Golovko 61)
3–0 (Shevchenko 72)
3–1 (Hughes 82)

Panathinaikos...................................1
Lens 0

1–0 (Vokolos 53)

25 November 1998

Arsenal..0
Lens 1

0–1 (Debeve 72)
(Parlour, Arsenal sent off 90)
(Vairelles, Lens sent off 90)

Dynamo Kiev....................................2
Panathinaikos...................................1

0–1 (Lagonikakis 36)
1–1 (Rebrov 72)
2–1 (Basinas 80 og)

9 December 1998

Lens 1
Dynamo Kiev 3

0–1 (Kaladze 60)
0–2 (Vashchuk 75)
1–2 (Smicer 78)
1–3 (Shevchenko 85)

Panathinaikos...................................1
Arsenal 3

0–1 (Boa Morte 65)
1–1 (Sypniewski 74)
1–2 (Anelka 80)
1–3 (Boa Morte 86)

Dynamic
Shevchenko

Kiev dynamoes

FINAL GROUP E TABLE

TEAMS	P	W	D	L	F	A	Pts
DYNAMO KIEV	6	3	2	1	11	7	11
LENS	6	2	2	2	5	6	8
ARSENAL	6	2	2	2	8	8	8
PANATHINAIKOS	6	2	0	4	6	9	6

Greek heroes foil Ajax

Olimpiakos make it, while Dutch champions slip to bottom

16 September 1998

Porto .2
Olympiakos 2
1–0 (Zahovic 65)
2–0 (Jardel 82)
2–1 (Giannakopoulos 86)
2–2 (Gogic 89)

Croatia Zagreb 0
Ajax 0

30 September 1998

Olympiakos 2
Croatia Zagreb 0
1–0 (Alexandris 22)
2–0 (Gogic 81)

Ajax 2
Porto 1
1–0 (Rudy 57)
1–1 (Zahovic 69)
2–1 (Litmanen 86 pen)

21 October 1998

Olympiakos 1
Ajax 0
1–0 (Alexandris 38, right)

Porto 3
Croatia Zagreb 0
1–0 (Junior 33)
2–0 (Zahovic 43)
3–0 (Zahovic 45)

4 November 1998

Ajax 2
Olympiakos 0
1–0 (Witschge 36)
2–0 (Gorre 88)

Croatia Zagreb 3
Porto 1
1–0 (Mikic 7)
2–0 (Rukavina 37)
2–1 (Jardel 39)
3–1 (Mujcin 61)

25 November 1998

Olympiakos 2
Porto 1
1–0 (Gogic 17)
2–0 (Djordjevic 55)
2–1 (Zahovic 76)

Ajax 0
Croatia Zagreb 1
0–1 (Simic 68)

9 December 1998

Porto 3
Ajax 0
1–0 (Zahovic 54)
2–0 (Zahovic 73)
3–0 (Drulovic 79)

Croatia Zagreb 1
Olympiakos 1
1–0 (Jelicic 35)
1–1 (Georgatos 64)

Ajax were huge favourites to win this group but in the end it was unfancied Olimpiakos of Greece who won through in some style. 2–0 down to Porto with five minutes left in their first game, Olimpiakos managed a morale-boosting draw, and hardly looked back, although a 2–0 defeat at Ajax meant that this group went to the wire.

In fact, as the teams kicked off for the last game, any one of three could have qualified, but Ajax crumbled away at Porto and Olimpiakos fought out a gutsy draw in Croatia to go through to the quarter-finals.

Despite being out of the running quite early on, it was Porto who produced the top scorer in the group, the Slovakian midfielder Zlatko Zahovic (right), who hit a total of seven goals.

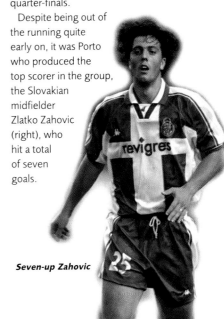

Seven-up Zahovic

Ajax boss, Morten Olsen turns his back on the table

FINAL GROUP A TABLE							
TEAMS	P	W	D	L	F	A	Pts
OLIMPIAKOS	6	3	2	1	8	6	11
CROATIA ZAGREB	6	2	2	2	5	7	8
PORTO	6	2	1	3	11	9	7
AJAX	6	2	1	3	4	6	7

The Old Lady sneaks through

The past masters make it to the quarters despite winning only one in six

Juventus, old hands at getting through to the latter stages of the Champions' League without setting the world alight, topped Group B despite winning only one game out of six – their last, against Rosenborg of Norway. To their credit, the Italians didn't lose a game either, managing to draw five times.

Athletic Bilbao, who qualified by coming third in the Spanish League, were always likely to be the whipping boys of this group, and were out of the running from early on. Galatasaray and Rosenborg were neck and neck at the top until the Italians' late surge saw them overtaken. In fact, if Galatasaray hadn't lost, surprisingly, to Bilbao in their last match, Juventus wouldn't have got through at all.

Unsurprisingly there wasn't a clear leading scorer in the group, with Sukur, Rushdfeldt and Inzaghi each bagging three apiece.

A hat-trick for Rushfeldt. . .

16 September 1998

Athletic Bilbao 1
Rosenborg 1
1–0 (Etxeberria 6)
1–1 (Strand 65)

Juventus 2
Galatasaray 2
1–0 (Inzaghi 17)
1–1 (Sukur 44)
1–2 (Umit 63)
2–2 (Birindelli 68)
(Peruzzi, Juventus sent off 32)

30 September 1998

Galatasaray 2
Athletic Bilbao 1
1–0 (Okan 16)
1–1 (Urzaiz 17)
2–1 (Hagi 92)

Rosenborg 1
Juventus 1
0–1 (Inzaghi 27)
1–1 (Skammelsrud 69 pen)

21 October 1998

Rosenborg 3
Galatasaray 0
1–0 (Rushfeldt 68)
2–0 (Rushfeldt 86)
3–0 (Rushfeldt 90)

Athletic Bilbao 0
Juventus 0

4 November 1998

Galatasaray 3
Rosenborg 0
1–0 (Sukur 55)
2–0 (Arif 66)
3–0 (Sukur 74, right)

Juventus 1
Athletic Bilbao 1
0–1 (Guerrero 46)
1–1 (Lasa 69 og)

25 November 1998

Rosenborg 2
Athletic Bilbao 1
1–0 (Sorensen 2)
2–0 (Sorensen 50)
2–1 (Jorge Perez 91)

2 December 1998

Galatasaray 1
Juventus 1
0–1 (Amoruso 78)
1–1 (Kaya 90)

9 December 1998

Athletic Bilbao 1
Galatasaray 0
1–0 (Guerrero 44)

Juventus 2
Rosenborg 0
1–0 (Inzaghi 16, right)
2–0 (Amoruso 35)

FINAL GROUP B TABLE

TEAMS	P	W	D	L	F	A	Pts
JUVENTUS	6	1	5	0	7	5	8
GALATASARAY	6	2	2	2	8	8	8
ROSENBORG	6	2	2	2	7	8	8
ATHLETIC BILBAO	6	1	3	2	5	6	6

. . .and three for Inzaghi

Real and Inter finish on top

The southern Europeans show their class to both ease through

16 September 1998

Real Madrid 2
Inter 0
1–0 (Hierro 79 pen)
2–0 (Seedorf 90)
(Fresi, Inter sent off 42)

Sturm Graz.......................................0
Spartak Moscow.............................2
0–1 (Titov 60)
0–2 (Tsimbalar 64)

30 September 1998

Spartak Moscow.............................2
Real Madrid 1
0–1 (Raul 63)
1–1 (Tsimbalar 72)
2–1 (Titov 78)

Inter 1
Sturm Graz.......................................0
1–0 (Djorkaeff 94)

21 October 1998

Inter 2
Spartak Moscow.............................1
1–0 (Ventola 32)
2–0 (Ronaldo 59)
2–1 (Tsimbalar 65)

Real Madrid 6
Sturm Graz.......................................1
0–1 (Vastic 8)   *3-1 (Jarni 61)*
1–1 (Savio 13)   *4-1 (Popovic 67 og)*
2–1 (Raul 22)   *5-1 (Jarni 79)*
                       6-1 (Savio 93)

4 November 1998

Spartak Moscow.............................1
Inter 1
1–0 (Tikhonov 68)
1–1 (Simeone 89)

Sturm Graz.......................................1
Real Madrid 5
1–0 (Haas 3)
1–1 (Panucci 8)
1–2 (Mijatovic 35)
1–3 (Seedorf 57)
1–4 (Panucci 61)
1–5 (Suker 74)

25 November 1998

Inter 3
Real Madrid 1
1–0 (Zamorano 51)
1–1 (Seedorf 59)
2–1 (Baggio 86)
3–1 (Baggio 95)

Spartak Moscow.............................0
Sturm Graz.......................................0

9 December 1998

Real Madrid 2
Spartak Moscow.............................1
1–0 (Raul 34)
2–0 (Savio 66)
2–1 (Khlestov 89)

Sturm Graz.......................................0
Inter 2
0–1 (Zanetti 64)
0–2 (Baggio 80)

There were two heavyweights, one surprise package and a whipping boy in this group. The big boys were holders Real Madrid, and Inter Milan, with nine European Cups between them. Spartak Moscow were the dark horses, while Austrian champions Sturm Graz were the damp squibs.

The real turning point in the group was the last-minute equaliser in Moscow by Inter Milan's Diego Simeone, which prevented the Italians from dropping into third place in the group, three points behind the Russians with two games to play.

Real Madrid, despite losing twice, were the top scorers with 17 goals. Two players scored two, while Seedorf, Savio and Raul bagged three each. The group's other top scorers were Spartak's Tsimbalar and Inter's Roberto Baggio (above).

Real's Raul

FINAL GROUP C TABLE

TEAMS	P	W	D	L	F	A	Pts
INTER	6	4	1	1	9	5	13
REAL MADRID	6	4	0	2	17	8	12
SPARTAK MOSCOW	6	2	2	2	7	6	8
STURM GRAZ	6	0	1	5	2	16	1

Real Champions

Kaiserslautern win through

Two British-led teams lose out to the Germans

Benfica, coached by Graeme Souness, and Bobby Robson's PSV were the only teams with any European pedigree in this group, but in the end it was the German champions Kaiserslautern who won through and in some style.

It was two gutsy wins over PSV that really set the Germans on their way; they fought back from a goal down in each case to head the group. And a hat-trick from the former-Manchester City striker Uwe Rosler (who had fallen on better times) finally brought them qualification to the quarter-finals – heights they had never previously reached.

Benfica finished second, but never quite recovered from a disastrous double header (home draw, away defeat) against minnows Helsinki to press the Germans much. Top scorer was PSV's Ruud van Nistelrooy with five.

Souness recalls the good old days

16 September 1998

PSV Eindhoven 2
Helsinki 1
0–1 (Kottila 31)
1–1 (Ooijer 57)
2–1 (Bruggink 90)

Kaiserslautern 1
Benfica 0
1–0 (Wagner 41)

30 September 1998

Benfica 2
PSV Eindhoven 1
1–0 (Ribeiro 47)
1–1 (Rommedahl 70)
2–1 (Pinto 76)

Helsinki 0
Kaiserslautern 0

21 October 1998

Helsinki 2
Benfica 0
1–0 (Lehkosuo 19 pen)
2–0 (Kottila 68)

PSV Eindhoven 1
Kaiserslautern 2
1–0 (Khokhlov 57)
1–1 (Riedl 67)
1–2 (Rische 81)

4 November 1998

Benfica 2
Helsinki 2
0–1 (Minto 3 og)
1–1 (Ribeiro 80)
2–1 (Da Silva 81)
2–2 (Moraes 84)

Kaiserslautern 3
PSV Eindhoven 1
0–1 (van Nistelrooy 18)
1–1 (Rische 68)
2–1 (Reich 77)
3–1 (Hristov 91)

25 November 1998

Helsinki 1
PSV Eindhoven 3
0–1 (van Nistelrooy 30)
0–2 (van Nistelrooy 67)
1–2 (Lehkosuo 70 pen)
1–3 (van Nistelrooy 81 pen)

Benfica 2
Kaiserslautern 1
1–0 (Ribeiro 31)
2–0 (Pinto 70, right)
2–1 (Rische 90)

9 December 1998

PSV Eindhoven 2
Benfica 2
1–0 (Khokhlov 41)
1–1 (Ribeiro 47 pen)
1–2 (Ribeiro 65)
2–2 (van Nistelrooy 88)

Kaiserslautern 5
Helsinki 2
0–1 (Ilola 29)
1–1 (Rosler 43)
2–1 (Marschall 49)
3–1 (Rosler 61)
3–2 (Moraes 68)
4–2 (Rosler 80)
5–2 (Rische 85)

Rosler prefers it at Kaiserslautern

FINAL GROUP F TABLE

TEAMS	P	W	D	L	F	A	Pts
KAISERSLAUTERN	6	4	1	1	12	6	13
BENFICA	6	2	2	2	8	9	8
PSV EINDHOVEN	6	2	1	3	10	11	7
HELSINKI	6	1	2	3	8	12	5

CHAPTER 6

No quarter given

Becks gets revenge

Inter the melting pot

| QUARTER-FINAL First Leg | 3 March 1999 | Old Trafford | Att: 54,430 | Ref: H Krug (Germany) | Entertainment: 100% |

Manchester United 2 Inter Milan 0 United: Yorke 2

United had dug deep to battle through to the quarter-final stage, and they didn't have too long to wait before they found out who they were to play in the next round.

The Champions' League quarter-final draw was made in the Hotel International in Geneva on 16 December, with the matches scheduled for 3 and 17 March. Before the draw, United knew three things: as runners-up they had to play their first match at Old Trafford and they would not be facing Bayern Munich, from Group D, or Real Madrid, the other runner-up qualifiers.

The other teams in the draw were Dynamo Kiev, Juventus, Olimpiakos, Inter Milan and Kaiserslautern. Received wisdom was that the Italians and Dynamo Kiev were the teams to be avoided.

The first name drawn, to play Real Madrid, was Inter Milan. However this was against the rules (both were from Group C). Inter went back into the pot, and Dynamo Kiev were drawn out. The next team out would play Manchester United in the other home banker. Again Inter were drawn, this time the tie stood.

Next up was Juventus, the lucky Old Lady, pitted against surprise qualifiers Olimpiakos of Greece. Finally there was an all-German affair between Bayern Munich and Kaiserslautern. Of the four ties one stood out: the clash of Italian titans Inter and Manchester United, the richest club in the world.

To United's knowledgeable fans the draw immediately brought two thoughts to mind. The first was that Ronaldo 'the world's best player', the Brazilian phenomenon, a constant on the world's back pages and rarely off the small screen, was coming to Old Trafford. The other was that Diego Simeone, the Argentinian player who 'got Beckham sent off' in the World Cup, played for Inter. Revenge was in the air.

Bookmakers William Hill didn't like the look of the draw for United. They moved them from 3–1 favourites to win the competition to 4–1 joint second favourites, promoting Juventus to top spot. And, even though the tie was over two months away, Inter started the war of words through their defender Fabio Galante who stated, "Hooray, we're going to play the Spice Girls," before pouring scorn on United's defence.

Alex Ferguson was more diplomatic in his response. "It's an exciting draw, but a tough one too. Entertaining Inter and Ronaldo is another tremendous attraction and it's going to be another full-volume night at Old Trafford."

The intervening period between the pre-Christmas draw and the pre-spring first leg at Old Trafford had been kind to United and generally cruel to Inter. Ferguson's men were the right side of a 13-match unbeaten run which had included a 6–2 win at Leicester, an

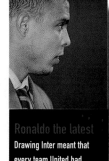

Ronaldo the latest

Drawing Inter meant that every team United had played so far contained at least one Brazilian. Lodz: Rodrigo Carbone; Barcelona: Rivaldo, Giovanni, Anderson; Bayern: Elber; Brondby: Vragel Da Silva; Inter: Ze Elias and, of course, Ronaldo. Whether the Brazilian superstar would play at Old Trafford was another thing altogether...

THE DRAW IN FULL

Real Madrid	v	Dynamo Kiev
Manchester United	v	Inter Milan
Juventus	v	Olimpiakos
Bayern Munich	v	Kaiserslautern

(Matches played 3 and 17 March 1999)

Inter coach Mircea Lucescu looks worried as his team trains at Old Trafford

About to go Inter battle. . .

8–1 annihilation of Nottingham Forest and they had overtaken Aston Villa to head the Premiership table. They were also in the quarter-finals of the FA Cup, with all their players fit to face the Italians.

Inter, on the other hand, were in turmoil. Their manager, former Romanian coach Mircea Lucescu, was in open dispute with some of his leading players; they had drifted to sixth place in Serie A having lost two and drawn one of their last three league fixtures without scoring a goal; they were virtually out of the Italian Cup after losing 2–0 at home to Parma, having had three men sent off, and, worst of all, their talismanic mainstay, Ronaldo, was still on the injury list with not one but two dodgy knees.

Indeed speculation over the Brazilian's fitness filled the papers and news bulletins in the days running up to the match. The Italians were sending differing health reports about the Brazilian, who had been declared fit to play in Inter's 0–0 draw against Juventus on the preceding Sunday but had actually refused, saying he was in too much pain. Medics at the San Siro had then ruled the attacker out of the running for Old Trafford, but manager Lucescu had said, "Ronaldo is very well. I am astonished by how well he is. He is working a lot right now. I don't know when he will be back. He must be playing soon, though."

At first Alex Ferguson refused to be drawn into the speculation, stating, "The only thing we're doing is preparing ourselves to play well in a tough match against formidable opposition. We'll continue to do that with or without Ronaldo in their ranks. It won't change our outlook on the game at all." Then, with increased will-he-won't-he speculation in the immediate run-up to the match he made a cryptic comment worthy of his former skipper Eric Cantona, in which he insinuated that he wasn't going to be fooled by Italian kidology; "When an Italian tells me it's pasta on the plate I check under the sauce to make sure."

The speculation didn't end when the Italian team flew in the day before the match minus the Brazilian. While news filtered through that he might arrive later on President Massimo

> ❝ **When an Italian tells me it's pasta on the plate I check under the sauce to make sure** ❞
>
> ALEX FERGUSON ON THE RONALDO WILL HE/WON'T HE CONTROVERSY

Moratti's private jet, UEFA threw in their three Eurosworth by stating that even if Ronaldo arrived an hour before kick-off, he would still be allowed to play. In the end, the closest United fans got to seeing the man their Inter counterparts nicknamed 'Il Fenomeno' was the lookalike that *Manchester United Magazine* cheekily hired to wander round outside the stadium on the afternoon of the match.

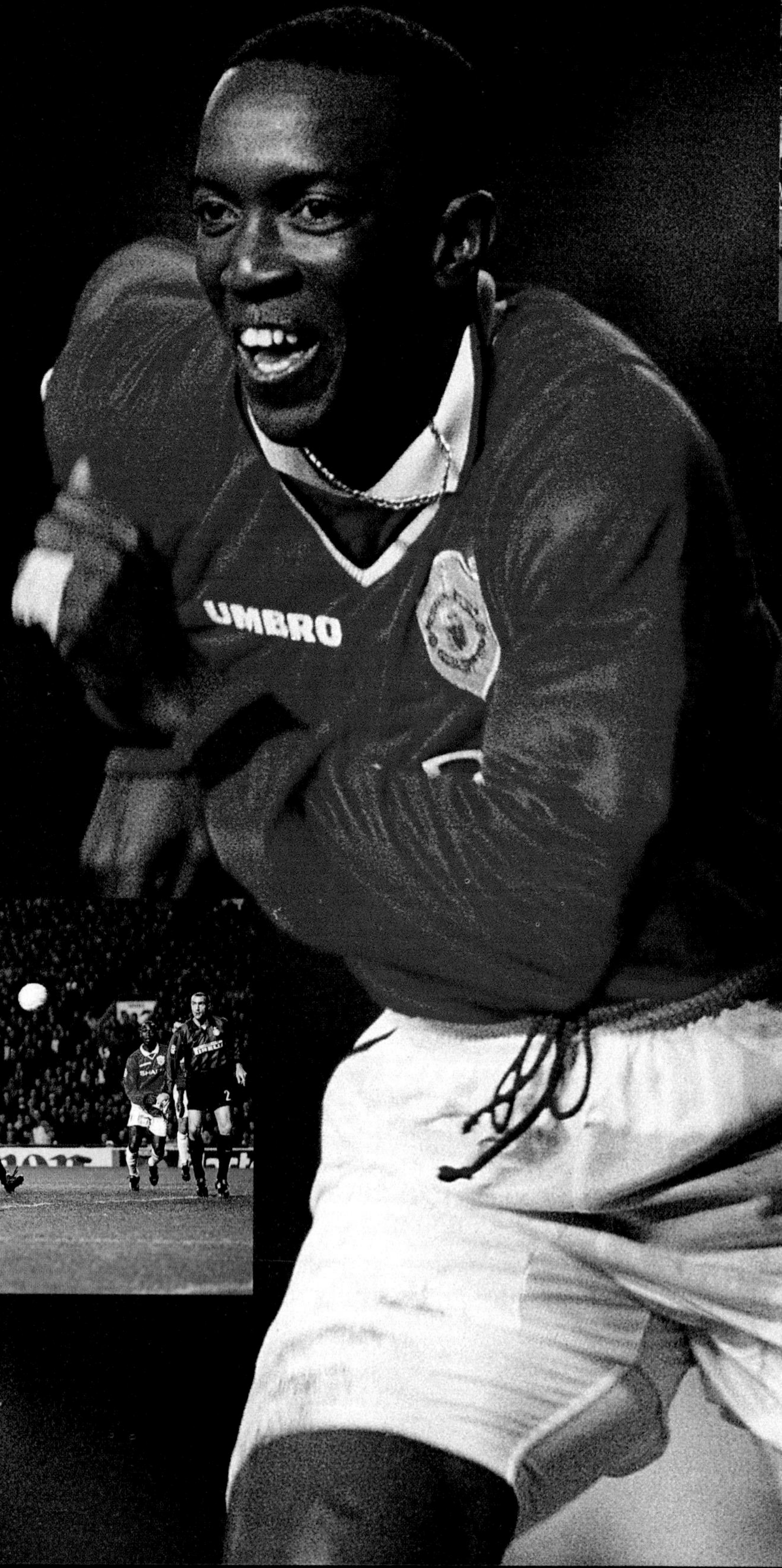
UMBRO

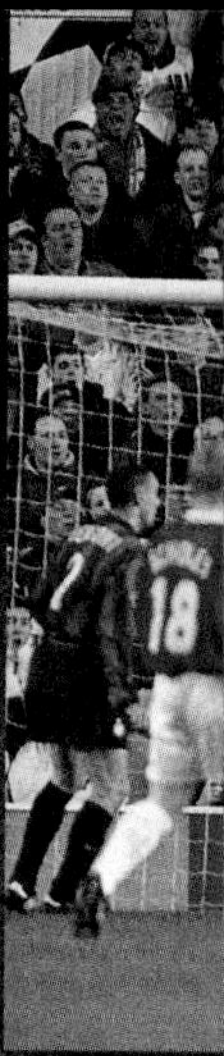

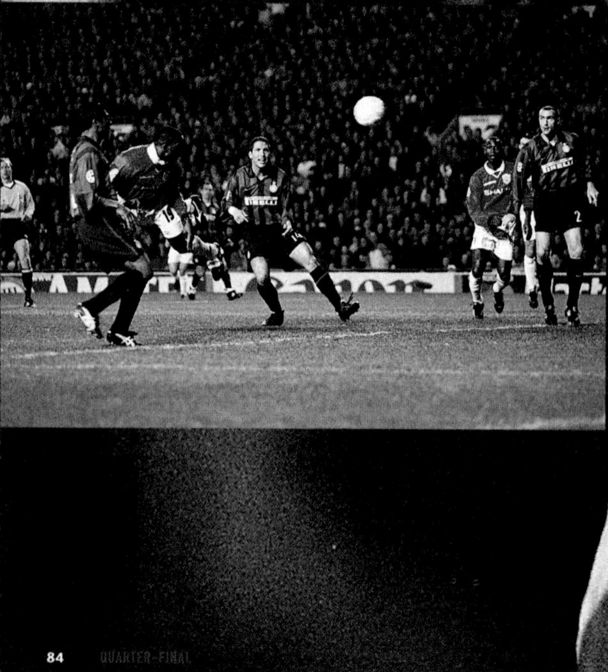

Beckham to Yorke, take one

❝ **Not losing a goal is vitally important for us. They will try and frustrate us, and catch us on the counter attack** ❞

ALEX FERGUSON

Ronaldo or no Ronaldo, Ferguson had been thorough in his preparations for the big game, boosted by having a full squad at his disposal for the first time at this stage of the competition. And, as usual, he warned against complacency. "Not losing a goal is vitally important for us. They will try and frustrate us, and catch us on the counter attack. This Inter team are a throwback to the Italian mentality where the result matters, nothing else."

The Theatre of Dreams erupted as the players marched onto the pitch to a backdrop of flares lit by the Inter Ultras in the East Stand. Much of the pre-match hype concerned Simeone and Beckham, looking forward to the first clash between the two since the Englishman's sending off in the World Cup. The two exchanged a stern handshake before the game, though Beckham didn't look the Argentinian in the eye. Then the battle commenced.

United tore at Inter from the start. On two minutes Beckham sent in a warning for the Italians in the shape of a dipping 30-yard free kick just over the bar, on five minutes he delivered a dipping cross which led to United taking the lead. From the left wing Scholes found Keane just inside the Inter half. Keane turned, worked out his options, and laid a trademark diagonal ball to the edge of the box searching out Yorke. Bergomi managed to intercept, but the ball bobbled into the air, and Yorke directed a header out wide to Beckham and made a run. Beckham hit the ball as only he knows how; first time, hard and accurate. Yorke, unmarked as Galante had left him to pressurise Beckham, dived to score with some aplomb against Gianluca Pagliuca, his sixth European goal in seven matches.

Inter fired back minutes later, when Simeone, fed by Zanetti, found the space to blast a 20-yarder at the United goal, but United came closer with a brilliant move which Pagliuca only just managed to keep out. Gary Neville started things off, throwing the ball to Yorke and belting down the wing for the return. His quick, low cross was beaten out by two Inter players, and the ball went spinning out of the box, into midfield, on the right flank. The last person Inter wanted to be there was Beckham, hanging back to cover for Neville. Beckham hit a looping cross into the box to meet a run between two defenders by Andy Cole. Cole stuck out his right leg to hit the ball towards the goal, but Pagliuca stuck out his left and diverted the ball past the post.

The best crosser of the ball in the world had found his range, however, and in first-half injury time, Pagliuca was unable to stop United scoring a second. Gary Neville spotted Beckham's overlapping run down the right and laid the ball into his path. Beckham had seen Yorke make a run into the box and aimed another wicked cross

85

Now you know...
Inter last won the European Cup back in 1965

towards him, even though the Tobagan was surrounded by a tangle of Italian defenders, including Pagliuca. However the keeper didn't come out, the defenders didn't jump, and Yorke hit the back of their net. Galante's taunts about the United defence's lack of quality were looking rather ironic. 2–0, and United's trudge to the dressing room was considerably lighter of step than Inter's.

Within a minute of the restart United should have scored a third. Yorke was the provider this time, running through two Italians before delivering a precise cross to Ryan Giggs who had stolen in on the far post, forgotten by his marker. Six yards out, the goal gaping, Giggs had time to pick his spot. He guided his header well wide of the post. Afterwards his body language, all head in hands and grim expression, said it all. He could have wrapped the tie up for United.

If the first half was all about United tearing into Inter, the second was all about Inter trying to get their own back. Or at least score an all-important away goal. While 2–0 was a great result for United 2–1 would have given the Italians the edge. They were to go close, incredibly close, on several occasions and on 60 minutes only a stunning Schmeichel save stopped a goal. Winter had the ball out on the left wing, but was finding difficulty getting rid of it due to pressure from Gary Neville. Beckham decided to join in, which left Galante, who had been marking him, free. Winter found the centre back, on the wing of all places, with a reverse pass and Galante thumped in a cross. Zamorano, who had got five yards goalside of Giggs, flung himself at the ball, meeting it with his head on the edge of the six-yard box. Schmeichel did a star jump, then, seeing the ball about to fly past his arm, moved it up and stopped a sure-fire goal. It was a remarkable save – half reaction, half technique – which very possibly kept United in the competition.

United retorted with a move of quality which was kept out more by luck than design by Dutchman Winter. Keane in midfield looked, as ever, for Yorke, saw him to his right and gave him the ball. Yorke gave it back and started on a run down the wing. Keane passed the ball back to him again, and the forward dribbled through two defenders, got to the byline, and laid a

daisy-cutter across to Cole, waiting at the far post. Cole looked certain to score, but thumped his shot into Winter's leg and the danger was cleared.

Inter, as they had to, fought back and won a corner on the right. Roberto Baggio hit it into the mixer and, agonisingly for United fans, Simeone thumped in a header. The agony turned to ecstacy, however, when the referee disallowed the goal. He had seen Galante drag down Henning Berg who was shaping to challenge for the ball and ordered a free kick. Simeone's goal celebrations turned into a mourning ritual as he knelt on the floor with his head in his hands.

It was United's turn to hit back in what was turning out to be a magnificent game. First, after some nice combination work by Keane and Yorke, Giggs hit a 20-yard drive that Pagliuca theatrically palmed over the bar. Then, picking up a clearance by the heroic Henning Berg, David Beckham delivered a Hoddlesque cross-field ball from his own half to Cole, who had got in front of his marker on the right. Fighting off a muscular challenge from Colonnese, in a scuffle that left the Italian flat on his backside, Cole reached the byline and crossed the ball towards Yorke, waiting on the far post. Pagliuca just got his fingertips in the way, and another chance was cleared.

Inter brought Ventola on for Zamorano and the youngster's pace began causing United problems. First Simeone laid a straight ball in his path from midfield, which split the United defence. Ventola got goalside of Berg, shook off a tug of the shirt and shaped to

"Ryan Giggs, Ryan Giggs flying down the wing"

66 I would have been happy with 1–0, so 2–0 was a pretty good result. I don't think it is over and we still have a lot of hurdles to face. But I think we will score over there and that gives us a great chance 99

ALEX FERGUSON

Beckham to Yorke, take two

No go Diego

66 I thought it was a goal for sure. It would have changed the whole complexion of the game. But it is not over yet 99

INTER COACH MIRCEA LUCESCU

shoot. Schmeichel, however, had made himself big, and his outstretched leg saved the day, deflecting the shot. Then, with seconds remaining, another ball from the midfield, this time from Cauet, reached Ventola again. This time it was Stam's turn to be outpaced by the youngster, but again Schmeichel spread himself superbly, again he blocked the shot.

The rebound, however, fell kindly for Inter, finding Colonnese on the edge of the box. Schmeichel picked himself up to charge at the Italian defender, who skilfully sidestepped him, and hit a shot at the goal. Berg, seeing his goalkeeper exposed, had taken position on the line and he stuck out his leg to, miraculously, keep the ball out. United had a two-goal cushion to take to Milan. But only just.

Friends again

After the match David Beckham achieved a public relations coup by approaching Diego Simeone, embracing him, and swapping shirts with him. The Argentinian's shirt was given, like all Beckam's others, to his father, who has built up quite a collection.

> 66 **Beckham was outstanding. He distinguished himself among some wonderful players** 99
>
> ALEX FERGUSON

MANCHESTER UNITED — 2

HOME TEAM	GOALS mins	ASSISTS mins	SHOTS ON	SHOTS OFF	SUB'D mins
1 PETER SCHMEICHEL					
5 RONNY JOHNSEN					46
6 JAAP STAM					
2 GARY NEVILLE					
3 DENIS IRWIN					
16 ROY KEANE			1		
7 DAVID BECKHAM		6, 45	2		
18 PAUL SCHOLES			1		69
11 RYAN GIGGS			1	3	
19 DWIGHT YORKE	6, 45		2	2	
9 ANDREW COLE			1		

SUBSTITUTES	GOALS mins	ASSISTS mins	SHOTS ON	SHOTS OFF	SUB'D for
17 RAI VAN DER GOUW					
8 NICK BUTT			2		#5
21 HENNING BERG					#18
12 PHIL NEVILLE					
15 JESPER BLOMQVIST					
20 OLE GUNNAR SOLSKJAER					
24 WES BROWN					

MATCH STATS
SHOTS ON TARGET 5   FOULS 22   OFFSIDES 1
SHOTS OFF TARGET 11   FREE KICKS 12   CORNER KICKS 4

UNITED'S RATING 91%

INTER MILAN — 0

AWAY TEAM	GOALS mins	ASSISTS mins	SHOTS ON	SHOTS OFF	SUB'D mins
1 GIANLUCA PAGLIUCA					
5 FABIO GALANTE					
2 GUISEPPE BERGOMI					
3 FRANCESCO COLONNESE					
4 JAVIER ZANETTI			3		
15 BENOIT CAUET			1		
14 DIEGO SIMEONE				2	
8 ARON WINTER					
10 ROBERTO BAGGIO					79
18 IVAN ZAMORANO			1		68
6 YOURI DJORKAEFF			1		

SUBSTITUTES	GOALS mins	ASSISTS mins	SHOTS ON	SHOTS OFF	SUB'D for
13 ZE ELIAS					
11 NICOLA VENTOLA			2		#18
25 MAURO MILANESE					
21 ANDREA PIRLO					#10
22 SEBASTIEN FREY					
16 TARIBO WEST					
27 DA SILVA GILBERTO					

MATCH STATS
SHOTS ON TARGET 7   FOULS 12   OFFSIDES 7
SHOTS OFF TARGET 3   FREE KICKS 22   CORNER KICKS 2

INTER'S RATING 68%

Flares before the flair

QUARTER–FINAL Second Leg   17 March 1999   San Siro   Att: 79,528   Ref: G Veissiere (France)   Entertainment: 80%

Inter Milan 1 Manchester United 1   Inter: Ventola   United: Scholes

Two things dominated the run-in to the second leg of the Champions' League quarter-final between United and Inter at the San Siro. The first was a war of words waged through the press after comments by Alex Ferguson. The second was, as ever, the question of the fitness of Inter's Brazilian striker Ronaldo. First off, the chin-wagging.

In a press conference in England a couple of days before the game, Ferguson, presumably in an attempt to pressurise the referee, stated of the Inter players, "I think there will be a lot of scheming, diving and referee-baiting. They will go through the whole repertoire of Italians at their best. I'm hoping it will be a good strong referee.

If we have that we have got a chance."

The response from Inter was furious. The Nerazzurri's Romanian manager, Mircea Lucescu, stated, "What he has said is a sad thing and a bad thing, but maybe he has done this because he is afraid," before jabbing in a little jibe himself. "I always believed in the English sense of fair play. But then Alex Ferguson is from Scotland, and they don't have fair play there, apparently."

Inter's Dutch midfielder Aron Winter also weighed in with a few comments, too. "Ferguson is looking for an alibi in case his team is beaten by us. We have no intention of using the kind of tactics he has said we will employ."

Pretty soon peace was brokered and the attention moved to Ronaldo, who had made something of a comeback, playing a half of

Where on Earth?

Milan, population 1.5 million, is the fashion capital of Europe. Lying in the shadow of the Alps, this northern Italian city houses the world famous Scala opera house.

"Inter who?"

Trouble flares among the Inter Ultras

Inter's derby against Milan the preceding Sunday. Inter had come back from being two goals down to equalise against their old foes, though Ronaldo hadn't scored. Fresh worries arose when the Brazilian didn't turn up for Monday morning's training session, complaining of a headache, though he did arrive later that afternoon. Such was the growing hysteria surrounding the player, even his migraine made international headlines.

Ronaldo insisted he was up to the big game. "Yes, I am ready," he told reporters. "I'm increasing my fitness little by little. Now I am happy, now I can say I am satisfied. It will be a decisive match with the whole season's work going into it. I am not afraid of the pressure, I am not afraid of the responsibility. Ronaldo has always lived with this pressure." You know things have started going wrong when people refer to themselves in the third person.

One hundred per cent fit or otherwise, Ronaldo's presence in the team was a boost to Inter. "Inter are very much improved by having him back," said Milan defender Thomas Helveg after playing against the Brazilian the weekend before. "He plays behind the striker and the other team needs two defenders looking after him, so if Inter play two wingers it is very difficult to control them all."

Despite alarming allegations by Portuguese international Paolo Sousa that Inter didn't have a game plan and no one knew what anyone else was doing on the pitch, which got him kicked out of the squad, Inter were to play an interesting variation of the 3-5-2 formation with Bergomi as a sweeper, West and Colonnese as central defenders, Zanetti and Silvestre as wing backs, Simeone and Cauet in central midfield and Baggio lying behind Ronaldo and Zamorano up front, leaving the likes of Ventola and Moriero itching on the bench.

Fergie relied on his classic 4-4-2 formation and, with a full-strength side, was adamant that United would not abandon their attacking policy, insisting they would score at least one goal and thus force the Italians to notch four, though he did play Ronny Johnsen in central midfield, leaving Scholes on the bench. The whole United camp had a confident, buoyant look about it, most of them undoubtedly blissfully unaware of the fact that over the last four decades, in six

"Please God, spare me from Jaap Stam"

Now you know...
United had never previously beaten an
Italian team in Italy

Stam 2 Inter 0

different ties, United had never beaten an Italian
side, had lost all their previous games in Italy and
scored just one goal.

The atmosphere in the San Siro as the players
ran onto the pitch, Ronaldo last in the illustrious
Inter line, made Old Trafford's encounter look
like a Tupperware party. Inter's Curva Nord
Ultras – the Boys – had been preparing for the
game and scores of flares engulfed the ground
in smoke as the teams posed for photos. The
four thousand-plus United fans with their flags,
banners and even a few flares of their own,
made as much noise as they could but were
drowned out by the 75,000 Italians.

The home fans were nearly silenced in the
first minute, however, when Roy Keane cracked
a shot wide of the post. Minutes later United
fashioned another great move when Giggs
dribbled towards the area and chipped in a
pass towards Dwight Yorke, making a run to the
far post. Yorke, who had got in front of Taribo
West – his hair blue for the occasion – lunged
for the ball, but agonisingly he could only direct
it into the side netting.

Then came the inevitable Inter deluge. Their
first major chance fell on 16 minutes: Roberto
Baggio laid a ball onto the elegant Cauet who
saw an intelligent diagonal run by Zamorano

across the box, stealing a couple of yards on
Henning Berg, and bearing down on goal.
Schmeichel made a lunge for the ball but ended
up grasping thin air as the Chilean pushed it to
his side. The goalkeeper was left blocking the
striker's path and Zamorano went down under
the challenge. Contact proved to be minimal,
but contact there was – United were lucky not
to concede a penalty.

Zamorano was proving a Sepp-Maier-sized
handful for the United defence and a nearly
identical Cauet ball minutes later was collected
by the Chilean, who had made a virtually
identical run, this time leaving Gary Neville in
his wake. With Berg closing
him down he shot
from a narrow
angle, but
Schmeichel is
rarely beaten
from narrow
angles and he
blocked it.

United's brilliant
wing-play had been
Inter's downfall in the
first game, but Inter
proved they could

"This way to the semis lads"

cause United problems in the same area in their next attack. Cauet found Baggio halfway into United's half and the man the Italian press were now calling 'the ex-ponytail' crafted a well-weighted ball down the wing, having spotted that Zanetti had outflanked Giggs, whose marking isn't quite up to his dribbling. Zanetti put in a Beckham-like first-time cross over Schmeichel, Simeone and Berg to the head of the diving Zamorano with the goal gaping in front of him. Or so it seemed. With the Inter fans beginning their celebration, Berg somehow got a shoulder-high foot to the ball and cleared the danger.

It was a brilliant piece of defending but a stern warning to United: Inter were so dominant, a goal looked imminent.

Next a Baggio corner was headed out of the box by Ronny Johnsen but ended up, via a poke by Giggs, at the feet of Zanetti. The wing back shaped to shoot, which made Giggs turn and jump to try to block with his back. Zanetti, however, feinted and in doing so created the space for a better shot, which he drilled the length of the box, beating Schmeichel, but not his post. Baggio collected the rebound and fashioned to shoot, but was ruled offside.

A United goal at this point looked out of the question, but to their credit the punch-drunk Reds created a chance of their own as the half wore on. Irwin found Yorke with a long clearance

> ❝ He was magnificent, the referee, that was the best you'll get. Top drawer ❞

ALEX FERGUSON

Ventola (below) scores to give Schmikes (right) the jitters

Now you know…
Paul Scholes' goal was only United's second ever in Italy

and the Tobagan, holding the ball up, saw a darting run down the left wing by Johnsen, who in a moment of madness was under the delusion he was Ryan Giggs. Johnsen hit a cross-box daisy-cutter to Cole, who had made a run into the box. Cole, with Colonnese marking him indecently closely, got a foot to the ball but hit it over Pagliuca and the bar into the Inter Ultras.

Normal service was resumed in the second half. A long ball by Zanetti, who was still doing his on-form-Beckham impression, was so accurately aimed at the surging Ronaldo that it hit him square on the back. Baggio picked up the rebound and for a moment the two produced the sort of move that had people drooling with anticipation at the start of the season. Ronaldo ran to the left of the box then suddenly darted right, losing Gary Neville in the process. Baggio slipped the ball into his path and he hit a quick and venomous shot. The ball would have whipped past Schmeichel and into the net if he hadn't shown his trademark sharp reactions to stick out his arm and block it.

Minutes later, Ronaldo again showed the sort of form that had made him world number one, with a devastating burst towards the United box where he played a quick one-two with Henning Berg (who was trying to stop Baggio from doing the same thing) to reach the penalty area. He then beat Gary Neville with a neat step-over and looked to be on for a shot at goal when suddenly he crumpled to the floor as if pole-axed by a chopping tackle.

Replays showed that there had been a Neville nudge, but Ronaldo's over theatrical reaction didn't persuade the referee, Frenchman Gilles Veissiere, who waved play on with a smile, ignoring the Brazilian's Italian gesticulations of dismay and disbelief. Perhaps Alex Ferguson's pre-match attempts to persuade the referee of the Italians' wily ways had hit home, or perhaps the referee was genuinely a strong man, but minutes later he turned down another penalty appeal right in front of the baying Inter Ultras. Zamorano collected a throw in from the right and ran across the field finding Ze Elias surging towards goal with a clever back heel. The Brazilian. inside the box, was faced by Berg and Stam, with Roy Keane coming in from the side. Keane shaped to tackle then pulled out: Ze Elias must have already committed himself to a dive because he went down and to United's dismay the referee blew his whistle, and started brandishing a yellow card. The yellow, however, was for the Brazilian rather than the Irishman, the kick went United's way, and justice was done.

Having failed to score through guile, the Italians employed skill to create the next real moment of danger on 63 minutes. Cauet picked up a powerful Jaap Stam header from a corner and bore down on goal. Ventola, just on for Ronaldo and fresh-legged, made a run into the box which Cauet spotted. He scooped a ball into the danger area which Keane attempted to clear

with an overhead kick. The United skipper made minimal contact with the ball, however, and the jubilant No 11 sidefooted it past Schmeichel. It was the least the Italians deserved, and the game was hanging in the balance. 1–0.

Inter continued their siege of United's goal, to try to force extra time. Their best chance fell with eight minutes to go. Cauet, as ever, was at the heart of the move, passing the ball to Baggio, who laid it off to Ze Elias. The Brazilian, spotting a Ventola run, attempted a pass to the youngster which was intercepted by a sliding Berg. Baggio picked up the ball then fell over the Norwegian's still-outstretched legs and the ball broke free to Ze Elias who suddenly found himself with a clear sight of goal from 15 yards out. But, with David Beckham closing in and Schmeichel narrowing the angle to perfection, the shot was hit with panic rather than precision and curled well wide of the post.

❝ I didn't see Scholes' goal go in. I had fainted by then ❞
ALEX FERGUSON

"Unlucky Ron son, see ya in the bar"

"Yeeeeaaaaaassss!"

Phil Neville: the most well-balanced player in the squad

Victory makes Keane feel ten-feet tall

Beck to the semis!

Possession was a rare commodity for United, so the last thing Scholes wanted to do with five minutes left was to lose the ball in midfield to Cauet. But the Inter player proved more determined and again found the menacing Baggio on the edge of United's box. Inter's No 10 held the ball up and laid it back to Cauet, who had spotted an unmarked run by substitute Moriero on the right. He laid a well-weighted ball into the path of the Italian international, who thumped a shot across the goal and wide.

United found their way off the ropes for a brief period and Yorke headed for the Italian corner flag in order to use up some precious time. Surrounded by furious Italians he changed his mind and passed the ball down the pitch to Gary Neville who had seen that, in their eagerness to retrieve possession, the Italians had left only one man in the box, Taribo West, to mark both Cole and Scholes. The Nigerian was stranded in no-man's land as Cole coolly headed Neville's curled cross into the path of United's No 18. Scholes kept his head and sidefooted the ball through Pagliuca into the back of the net. Even the most pessimistic United fan immediately relaxed. Inter now had to score three more goals in two minutes to win and the rest of the game was played to joyful choruses from the United 4,000. Their team had reached the semi-final of the competition for the fourth time in its history.

"You're not singing anymore"

> 66 I may need a triple bypass after that. I don't care who we get now. I am just so happy to get to the semi-finals. We could get Melchester Rovers and I wouldn't mind 99

ALEX FERGUSON

INTER MILAN — 1

HOME TEAM		GOALS mins	ASSISTS mins	SHOTS ON OFF	SUB'D mins
1	GIANLUCA PAGLIUCA				
3	FRANCESCO COLONNESE				
24	MICKAEL SILVESTRE				
2	GUISEPPE BERGOMI				69
16	TARIBO WEST				
4	JAVIER ZANETTI			3	
14	DIEGO SIMEONE				32
15	BENOIT CAUET		63	1	
10	ROBERTO BAGGIO			1	
9	RONALDO			1	59
18	IVAN ZAMORANO			1	

SUBSTITUTES		GOALS mins	ASSISTS mins	SHOTS ON OFF	SUB'D for
13	ZE ELIAS			3	#14
11	NICOLA VENTOLA	63		2	#9
17	FRANCESCO MORIERO			1	#2
22	SEBASTIEN FREY				
5	FABIO GALANTE				
8	ARON WINTER				
6	YOURI DJORKAEFF				

MATCH STATS

SHOTS ON TARGET	6	FOULS	17	OFFSIDES	4	**INTER'S RATING**
SHOTS OFF TARGET	7	FREE KICKS	16	CORNER KICKS	7	**77%**

MANCHESTER UNITED — 1

AWAY TEAM		GOALS mins	ASSISTS mins	SHOTS ON OFF	SUB'D mins
1	PETER SCHMEICHEL				
2	GARY NEVILLE				
3	DENIS IRWIN				
6	JAAP STAM				
21	HENNING BERG				
7	DAVID BECKHAM			3	
5	RONNY JOHNSEN				76
11	RYAN GIGGS				81
16	ROY KEANE			1 2	
9	ANDREW COLE		88	1 2	
19	DWIGHT YORKE			3	

SUBSTITUTES		GOALS mins	ASSISTS mins	SHOTS ON OFF	SUB'D for
17	RAI VAN DER GOUW				
12	PHIL NEVILLE			1	#11
18	PAUL SCHOLES	88			#5
10	TEDDY SHERINGHAM				
15	JESPER BLOMQVIST				
20	OLE GUNNAR SOLSKJAER				
24	WES BROWN				

MATCH STATS

SHOTS ON TARGET	6	FOULS	16	OFFSIDES	6	**UNITED'S RATING**
SHOTS OFF TARGET	7	FREE KICKS	17	CORNER KICKS	5	**82%**

Bayern cruise…

Bayern, runaway leaders in the Bundesliga, were favourites to beat last year's surprise German champions Kaiserslautern in this all-German quarter-final in the Olympic Stadium in Munich.

But, against the odds, it was Kaiserslautern who made the early running, creating three chances in the first half hour; Rosler and Rische headed wide and Wagner hit the bar with a free kick from outside the box. Then Bayern got into gear, Matthaus put in a cross which rebounded off Jancker to Elber who fired the ball into the net from close range. Then, on 35 minutes, Strunz's measured ball found Effenberg clear on goal and the blond international midfielder made no

mistake with his shot. The second half was virtually all Bayern, who were given added impetus when Ramzy was sent off on 71 minutes. They went close again through Elber and Tarnat, but couldn't score a third goal which would have made their passage through to the semis a formality.

Kaiserslautern get ready for beat your neighbour

3 March 1999 Quarter-final 1st leg
Bayern 2 Kaiserslautern 0

Olimpiastadion, Munich
Referee: N Levnikov (Russia)

BAYERN		KAISERSLAUTERN	
1	OLIVER KAHN	1	ANDREAS REINKE
2	MARKUS BABBEL	3	MICHAEL BALLACK
3	BIXENTE LIZARAZU	6	HANY RAMZY
8	THOMAS STRUNZ	8	MARTIN WAGNER
9	GIOVANE ELBER	10	CIRIACO SFORZA
10	LOTHAR MATTHAUS	12	MARCO REICH
11	STEFAN EFFENBERG	15	JANOS HRUTKA
14	MARIO BASLER	18	JURGEN RISCHE
16	JENS JEREMIES	20	UWE ROSLER
19	CARSTEN JANCKER	22	ANDREAS BUCK
25	THOMAS LINKE	23	THOMAS RIEDL
SUBSTITUTES		SUBSTITUTES	
22	BERND DREHER	25	LAJOS SZUCS
4	SAMUEL KUFFOUR	4	AXEL ROOS
5	THOMAS HELMER	5	SAMIR
18	MICHAEL TARNAT	17	RATINHO
20	HASAN SALIHAMIDZIC	19	OLIVER SCHAFER
21	ALEXANDER ZICKLER	24	HARRY KOCH
24	ALI DAEI	27	DANIEL GRAF

It's over and out for Kaiserslautern

...to rule Germany

17 March 1999 Quarter-final 2nd leg
Kaiserslautern 0 Bayern 4

Fritz-Walter Stadion, Kaiserslautern
Referee: U Meier (Switzerland)

KAISERSLAUTERN BAYERN

KAISERSLAUTERN		BAYERN	
1	ANDREAS REINKE	1	OLIVER KAHN
3	MICHAEL BALLACK	2	MARKUS BABBEL
8	MARTIN WAGNER	3	BIXENTE LIZARAZU
10	CIRIACO SFORZA	4	SAMUEL KUFFOUR
12	MARCO REICH	10	LOTHAR MATTHAUS
15	JANOS HRUTKA	11	STEFAN EFFENBERG
17	RATINHO	14	MARIO BASLER
18	JURGEN RISCHE	16	JENS JEREMIES
20	UWE ROSLER	19	CARSTEN JANCKER
23	THOMAS RIEDL	21	ALEXANDER ZICKLER
24	HARRY KOCH	25	THOMAS LINKE
SUBSTITUTES		**SUBSTITUTES**	
2	UWE GOSPODAREK	12	SVEN SCHEUER
4	AXEL ROOS	5	THOMAS HELMER
5	SAMIR	7	MEHMET SCHOLL
13	PASCAL OJIGWE	17	THORSTEN FINK
19	OLIVER SCHAFER	18	MICHAEL TARNAT
27	DANIEL GRAF	20	HASAN SALIHAMIDZIC
28	JUNIOR	24	ALI DAEI

Kaiserslautern's faint hopes of turning round a 2-0 deficit against Bayern Munich were dashed as early as the eighth minute when Janos Hrutka brought down Carsten 'the Tank' Jancker to give away a penalty and get sent off to boot.

Effenberg hit in the spot-kick, and Bayern went on to rout their compatriots in front of their own fans.

Six-foot five-incher Jancker was outstanding, doubling Bayern's score on 22 minutes with a header in from a cross by Lizarazu and adding a third five minutes before the break, with a deflected shot from ten yards. The second half, with Bayern's qualification a formality, was played at a slower pace, with 'Supermario' Basler finishing off the scoring on 56 minutes.

Jens the Interceptor

Evens in Madrid

Holders hold on

Tosh has a Real job on his hands

Suker punch

Recently re-appointed Real Madrid manager John Toshack (Real's sixth boss in three-and-a-half years) maintained his proud record of never having lost at the Bernebeu – but only just – and the resulting home draw left Kiev favourites to reach the semis.

In truth Real should have wrapped the game up in the first half with Raul particularly profligate and Mijatovic and Morientes also spurning good chances. But Andrei Shevchenko showed why Milan were after him, maintaining his fine Champions' League form and threatening to score either side of half time, before finally breaking through in the 56th minute. Ten minutes later Mijatovic, scorer of the goal which brought the Champions' League title to Real last year, scored a magnificent free kick to equalise. The Spanish dominated possession thereafter, but Shevchenko and co always looked the more likely to score.

3 March 1999 Quarter-final 1st leg
Real Madrid 1 Dynamo Kiev 1
Santiago Bernebeu Stadium, Madrid
Referee: A Frisk (Germany)

REAL MADRID	DYNAMO KIEV
1 BODO ILLGNER	1 OLEX SHOVKOVSKI
2 CHRISTIAN PANUCCI	2 OLEH LUZHNYI
3 ROBERTO CARLOS	4 OLEX HOLOVKO
4 FERNANDO HIERRO	5 VLADYSLAV VASCHUK
5 MANUEL SANCHIS	7 KAKHA KALADZE
6 FERNANDO REDONDO	9 VITALEI KOSSOVSKYI
7 RAUL	10 ANDREI SHEVCHENKO
8 PREDRAG MIJATOVIC	11 SERGI REBROV
10 CLARENCE SEEDORF	14 ANDREI HUSIN
14 GUTI	15 ALEX KHATSKEVICH
15 FERNANDO MORIENTES	24 VALIANTSIN BIALKEVICH
SUBSTITUTES	**SUBSTITUTES**
13 PEDRO CONTRERAS	12 VIACH KERNOZENKO
9 DAVOR SUKER	3 ALEXEI GUERASSIMENKO
11 SAVIO	17 SERGI FEDOROV
12 IVAN CAMPO	18 VASSYL KARDASH
16 JAIME	19 DMYTRO MYKHAILENKO
17 ROBERT JARNI	23 OLEX KIRIUKHIN
22 CHRISTIAN KAREMBEU	31 SERGI KORMILTSEV

Kiev go through

Toshack tastes defeat as Shevchenko nets twice

Champions' League holders Real Madrid fought hard but were ultimately dumped out of this year's competition by in-form Dynamo Kiev. Real, playing in sub-zero temperatures they weren't used to, nevertheless dominated the first half of the second leg, but couldn't turn their superiority into advantage.

The Ukrainians needed two goals to kill the tie off, and their cause was helped on 63 minutes when Shevchenko, put through by substitute Bialkevich, was brought down for a penalty. Shevchenko shattered the 80,000 crowd by hitting his shot straight at keeper Bodo Illgner, but was quick enough to net the rebound to turn their dismay into rapture.

With Real threatening a goal that would put the tie into extra time, Shevchenko struck again from close range with ten minutes to go. "It was an incredible game; we dominated for 90 minutes," complained Toshack afterwards. "Still, you can't win the European Cup every year." Quite.

That man again, Shevchenko

**17 March 1999 Quarter-final 2nd leg
Dynamo Kiev 2 Real Madrid 0**

*Olimpiski Stadium, Kiev
Referee: S Braschi (Italy)*

DYNAMO KIEV	REAL MADRID
1 OLEX SHOVKOVSKI	1 BODO ILLGNER
2 OLEH LUZHNYI	2 CHRISTIAN PANUCCI
4 OLEX HOLOVKO	3 ROBERTO CARLOS
5 VLADYSLAV VASCHUK	4 FERNANDO HIERRO
7 KAKHA KALADZE	5 MANUEL SANCHIS
9 VITALEI KOSSOVSKYI	6 FERNANDO REDONDO
10 ANDREI SHEVCHENKO	7 RAUL
11 SERGI REBROV	10 CLARENCE SEEDORF
14 ANDREI HUSIN	12 IVAN CAMPO
15 ALEX KHATSKEVICH	15 FERNANDO MORIENTES
18 VASSYL KARDASH	17 ROBERT JARNI
SUBSTITUTES	SUBSTITUTES
12 VIACH KERNOZENKO	9 DAVOR SUKER
17 SERGI FEDOROV	13 PEDRO CONTRERAS
22 SERGI KONOVALOV	14 GUTI
23 OLEX KIRIUKHIN	16 JAIME
24 VALIANTSIN BIALKEVICH	18 AITOR KARANKA
30 ARTEM YASHKIN	19 FERNANDO SANZ
31 SERGI KORMILTSEV	22 CHRISTIAN KAREMBEU

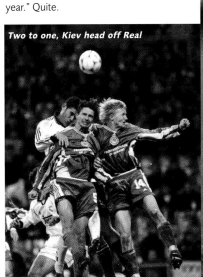

Two to one, Kiev head off Real

Careless hands

Old Lady robbed by Greeks

*My goal was **this** important*

**3 March 1999 Quarter-final 1st leg
Juventus 2 Olympiakos 1**

*Stadio Delle Alpi, Turin
Referee: J Aranda (Spain)*

JUVENTUS	OLYMPIAKOS
1 ANGELO PERUZZI	31 DIMI ELEFTHEROPOULOS
3 ZORAN MIRKOVIC	3 KYRIAKOS KARATAIDIS (C)
4 PAOLO MONTERO	5 GEORGIOS AMANATIDIS
7 ANGELO DI LIVIO	6 ILIAS POURSANIDIS
8 ANTONIO CONTE	7 STY GIANNAKOPOULOS
9 FILIPPO INZAGHI	9 SINICA GOGIC
11 DANIEL FONSECA	11 PREDRAG DJORDJEVIC
13 MARK IULIANO	14 DIMI MAVROGENIDIS
14 DIDIER DESCHAMPS	18 VASILIOS KARAPIALIS
21 ZINEDINE ZIDANE	21 GRIGORIOS GEORGATOS
26 EDGAR DAVIDS	32 GEORGIOS ANATOLAKIS
SUBSTITUTES	SUBSTITUTES
12 MICHEL RAMPULLA	1 KY TOHOUROGLOU
15 ALEX BIRINDELLI	4 ANDREAS NINIADIS
16 NICOLA AMORUSO	8 LUCIANO DE SOUZA
18 JOCELYN BLANCHARD	10 ILIJA IVIC
19 IGOR TUDOR	2 KOFI AMPONSAH
20 ALESSIO TACCHINARDI	25 PARASKEVAS ANTZAS
34 JUAN ESNAIDER	30 ALEXIOS ALEXANDRIS

Until well into stoppage time Juventus looked like they had done enough to negotiate their way into the semi-finals, leading 2–0 despite missing a number of sitters.

In the first half Filippo Inzaghi was the main culprit, missing the target on a number of occasions before finally putting the Old Lady ahead on 38 minutes. In the second 45 minutes, Zinedine Zidane should have scored twice before skipper Antonio Conte gave the fans something to cheer about with a cracker, 11 minutes from time.

But the away-goal rule makes the difference between 2–0 and 2–1 huge and the balance of the tie swung in the Greeks' favour when Juve keeper Angelo Peruzzi brought down Olympiakos sub Alexios Alexandris in the box after the Greek midfielder had skipped round him. Andreas Niniadis, another sub, slotted the last-gasp kick home to give the Greeks more than a chink of hope in the return.

Ivic gets out the wrong side of Ed

Out for the Conte

Juventus go through in last-gasp thriller

17 March 1999 Quarter-final 2nd leg
Olympiakos 1 Juventus 1
OAKA Spiros Louis Stadium, Athens
Referee: M Merk (Germany)

OLYMPIAKOS	JUVENTUS
31 DIMI ELEFTHEROPOULOS	1 MICHEL RAMPULLA
3 KYRIAKOS KARATAIDIS (C)	3 ZORAN MIRKOVIC
5 GEORGIOS AMANATIDIS	4 PAOLO MONTERO
6 ILIAS POURSANIDIS	7 ANGELO DI LIVIO
7 STY GIANNAKOPOULOS	8 ANTONIO CONTE (C)
9 SINICA GOGIC	9 FILIPPO INZAGHI
11 PREDRAG DJORDJEVIC	13 MARK IULIANO
14 DIMI MAVROGENIDIS	14 DIDIER DESCHAMPS
18 VASILIOS KARAPIALIS	21 ZINEDINE ZIDANE
21 GRIGORIOS GEORGATOS	26 EDGAR DAVIDS
32 GEORGIOS ANATOLAKIS	34 JUAN ESNAIDER
SUBSTITUTES	SUBSTITUTES
1 KY TOHOUROGLOU	12 MORGAN DE SANCTIS
4 ANDREAS NINIADIS	11 DANIEL FONSECA
8 LUCIANO DE SOUZA	15 ALEX BIRINDELLI
10 ILIJA IVIC	16 NICOLA AMORUSO
2 KOFI AMPONSAH	18 JOCELYN BLANCHARD
25 PARASKEVAS ANTZAS	19 IGOR TUDOR
30 ALEXIOS ALEXANDRIS	20 ALESSIO TACCHINARDI

Leading Juventus on away goals, Olympiakos were five minutes from sending Athens crazy and reaching the European Cup semi-finals for the first time in their history.

A late goal in Turin had handed them a lifeline a fortnight before and, in front of 70,000 passionate fans, an early goal when Sinica Gogic headed past Peruzzi from a Grigorios Georgatos cross looked enough to put them into the next round.

Peruzzi had blundered late on in the opening match, and it was his counterpart Dimi Eleftheropoulos who handed Juve the chance to qualify for their fourth successive Champions' League semi – Antonio Conte pounced after a handling error by the keeper and the Italians were through. "We leave this competition with our heads up" said Olympiakos manager Dujan Bajeric afterwards. "We deserved victory, creating the chances to score more goals, but missing them."

Goooalazzo!!!

CHAPTER **7**

One stop from Barcelona

Juventus arrive to hold up the United train

Old Lady mugs Reds

Manchester United 1 Juventus 1 United: Giggs Juventus: Conte

Before the home leg in the quarter-finals against Inter, United were waiting to see if a half-fit Ronaldo would turn up to Old Trafford. A month on, another home clash against Italian opponents and another will-he-won't-he-play situation over a world-class player with dodgy knees. This time Juventus were the opposition and World Player of the Year Zinedine Zidane was the crock in question.

Despite veiled threats from the boys upstairs at Juventus, Zidane had opted to play for France in the European Championship in March and had further injured his iffy joint, returning to Juventus with his leg in a brace. The Frenchman had been given intensive physio treatment since, and hadn't played in his club's pre-Old Trafford 1–0 defeat against Empoli, after which Juventus manger Carlo Ancelotti had said his inclusion or otherwise would be a "late decision".

Earlier in the season Juventus had been a club in some disarray, first losing their talismanic striker Alessandro Del Piero to long-term injury, then their manager Marcello Lippi, who had resigned after a run of bad results. Carlo Ancelotti, however, had won over the fans after early rejection (Lippi was much-loved) and had helped Juve regain much of the prowess expected of them. Indeed, Zidane or no

Yellow peril
The entire central midfield of both teams – Keane, Scholes, Deschamps (above) and Davids – started the game on a yellow card.

Zidane, the team likely to face United was an in-form one brimful of international stars: Italian No 1 Peruzzi in goal; top stopper Iuliano and Uruguayan hard-man Montero ruling the centre of defence; Mirkovic and Pessotto classy and fast on either flank; Conte, Deschamps, Davids and Di Livio providing a hard but skilful midfield and Pippo Inzaghi in-form up front. "Not a champagne Juventus," as Ancelotti put it, "but a very good one nonetheless." Their tactics were much like United's under Ferguson: 4-4-2, with Zidane (if available) playing the Cantona role just behind the striker.

United, remarkably, had no injuries or suspensions to worry about. "For us every player is fit, and that's quite amazing. You always expect one or two to carry knocks at this stage in the season. I'm very pleased about that. It's called luck," said Ferguson, whose only concern was midfield and whether to play the creative Scholes in the centre alongside Keane, or to employ a more defensive player – Butt or Johnsen – to stifle the Italians. "I've given a lot of thought to picking my right team. Possibly, Manchester United in the past never had a reputation for being defensive, but you can do this in a positive way if you use the right type of player in the right area of the field," he stated before the game, typically playing his cards close to his chest.

Ferguson, who had been fined £2,000 by UEFA after his comments before the Inter game, was less bellicose in his pre-match statements this time round, although he did throw out a little jab at the Juventus manager. "Ancelotti is a young coach and everyone has their own views on football. He has brought freshness and stability to Juventus after some bad results, but Lippi's experience is something I am glad I don't have to face." Even when prompted by an Italian journalist to repeat his comments about the Machiavellian nature of Italian players, he didn't react, responding instead, "You get so serious about these things. It was only a bit of fun, but it

UNITED AND JUVENTUS HEAD TO HEAD

1976 UEFA CUP
United 1–0 Juve
Juve 3–0 United
1984 CUP-WINNERS' CUP
United 1–1 Juve
Juve 2–1 United

1996 CHAMPIONS' LEAGUE
Juve 1–0 United
United 1–0 Juve
1997 CHAMPIONS' LEAGUE
United 3–2 Juve
Juve 1–0 United

Flying Dutchmen Jaap Stam and Edgar Davids get stuck in early doors

> **Ancelotti is a young coach and everyone has their own views on football. He has brought freshness and stability to Juventus after some bad results, but Lippi's experience is something I am glad I don't have to face**
>
> ALEX FERGUSON

obviously upset someone. You want to know what I think, but do you want to pay my fine?"

In response, Ancelotti threw in a little insult at United: "I said to Inzaghi, 'if you don't score against the English I'll never look you in the face again.'" But compared to the Inter war of words this was merely a skirmish as the old foes shaped up to play each other in the competition for the third time in three seasons. Midfielder Angelo Di Livio was actually complimentary about the Reds and stated, "The only real thrashing we have had in the last five years was the one we got at Old Trafford last season," before adding with a smile, "At least my daughter will be happy. She's a Spice Girls fan."

There wasn't much time for joking once the two teams ran on to another huge reception at Old Trafford, with the Italian fans again making their unique contribution to proceedings with flares, banners and chants. And, after a brief opening flurry by the home team, for much of the first half it was the Juve fans who had more cause to sing than those cheering on United.

With Juventus notably tighter at the back and quicker in the tackle than their Inter neighbours,

United were finding it very difficult to find space in attack or midfield and Zidane, who was playing with a heavily bandaged right leg, might have scored as early as the first minute had he taken more time with a 25-yard chip that went over the bar as well as Schmeichel. Cole responded with a header past the post from a Keane cross, but Juventus were running the game in midfield and very nearly scored in their next attack.

Zidane, playing deep, flighted a long ball towards the area where Berg was marking Inzaghi. The Norwegian, who might have headed away, let the ball bounce and the Italian beat him on the turn, cracking in a left foot shot that Schmeichel superbly saved at full stretch.

Yorke responded with a shot-on-the-turn of his own which finished over the bar but was offside anyway, then more rare pressure from United provided a free kick in Beckham-territory after Deschamps was harshly adjudged to have brought down Cole on the edge of the box. Giggs and Beckham had a little conference over who would take it, but there was never much doubt as to the outcome. If the No 7's precisely curled ball, which flashed past the wall and beat the

Now you know...
In 36 years, Juventus have only failed to
qualify for Europe once – in 1991.

keeper, had finished a millimetre to the right of
the post rather than the left United would have
been in front. It was so close that many fans
thought that they were. It was a rare positive
contribution to the first half from Beckham,
who found himself shackled on the right by Di
Livio just as Giggs was on the right by Pessotto.
If the Old Trafford wings were United's killing
fields against Inter, Juventus had them carefully
mined. To make matters worse Keane was man-
marking Zinedine Zidane, which left Scholes
overwhelmed in the centre of the park.

With Deschamps and Davids thus
running the show in midfield, and
Zidane getting plenty of possession
in his free role in the hole, despite Keane's
attention, Juventus continued to dominate the
first half, stringing passes together and
frustrating United into errors on the rare
occasions they got the ball. On 25 minutes, the
Italians' possession was rewarded with a goal;
typically it was scored after a precise series of
passes. Conte picked up a Stam header outside
the box, dribbled through a couple of United
midfielders and laid the ball square to Di Livio
in the left-wing position. The Italian
international played a lovely reverse pass to
Zidane in front of
him; the

Spot the ball

Frenchman brushed off a Berg challenge before
laying a square ball to Davids outside the box,
faced by Scholes. Now for the clever bit. Keane
left Juve skipper Conte to back up his team-
mate and Davids played the ball through
Scholes' legs to where the Irishman had been.
Conte, free, had time to turn before shooting,
left-footed past Schmeichel. It was no more
than the Italians deserved.

In yet another attack soon after, Inzaghi got an
earful from his team-mates after missing a
glorious chance to put Juventus virtually out of
sight (if there's such a thing against United).
Receiving a Davids' chip on the byline to the
right of the goal, he cut in, drew Schmeichel
and, with Conte and Zidane waiting to
pass his roll-back into an empty net,
tried a shot. He should have known
better; you don't beat the Dane on his
near post.

United started rallying towards the
end of the first half – a determined Giggs
run and a great cross from the left saw Cole
head over, while a Keane shot flashed wide
after nice approach play by Neville, Yorke and
Scholes. But it was Juventus who came closest
to scoring with a brilliant piece of counter-
attacking before the break. A Keane ball deep
in Juve territory was intercepted by Pessotto
who passed to Zidane and carried on his run.
Remember him. Zidane found Deschamps via

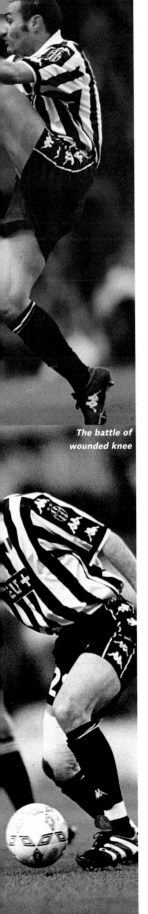

The battle of
wounded knee

> 66 **My instinct was that I was half-a-yard offside, but I've headed it, the ball's gone in, I've looked round at the linesman, and he's kept his flag down, so I've started celebrating. He must have taken six seconds to put the flag up** 99
>
> TEDDY SHERINGHAM

Edgar Davids and the Frenchman carefully weighted a ball into the box to the completely unmarked... Pessotto. The defender had time to take two touches before carefully curling a shot wide of the post. It was a let-off, and United knew it. And that wasn't all: Juventus had time for another chance before the interval, Inzaghi poking the ball wide from a right-wing cross from Zidane. The Frenchman, despite his injury, had been delivering a masterclass to United, running the show completely, demonstrating again what he had shown without doubt in the World Cup Final, that he, rather than Ronaldo, is the world's best player.

The first half over, and United had been given a lesson in football by their old European adversary, the Old Lady. In the second, they came out with a more determined look and from the off their interpassing looked neater and quicker, as it had to be against the hard-pressing Juventus players. In the first attack of the half, Scholes intercepted the ball, found Cole and the No 9 blasted the ball over. Next it was Scholes' turn. He received the ball outside the box after slick interplay by Beckham and Yorke only to hit it just over the bar. This was more like it. Soon after United won a corner. Beckham, of course, whipped it in, Giggs made a near-post run, and glanced in a powerful header. The surprised Peruzzi somehow beat it out.

Then United's best move of the game so far. Scholes received the ball after the breakdown of a Juventus attack, and a slick one-touch passing movement followed which saw Keane, Yorke and Scholes again involved before the ball fell to Cole on the left. He ran shoulder to shoulder into the box with Iuliano in close attendance, the Italian couldn't stop the Englishman from shooting, but the shot, again, went over. United's movement, with Keane

playing a much more active part, was improving as the match went on, and another slick move ended with the United skipper belting in a low shot from outside the area that Peruzzi was grateful to scoop up. Then Cole picked the ball up, again on the left, and slid in a cross to the penalty box that Giggs hit first time. The ball was blocked by Iuliano's right hand, Scholes picked up the rebound and fired wide. If the red-haired midfielder had left it alone, perhaps the referee would have given a penalty. As it was the United players were left protesting, and indeed, most refs would have given it in the circumstances. Manuel Diaz Vega, a Champions' League veteran with a final under his belt, didn't.

United, inevitably, were leaving spaces, and Juventus nearly capitalised. Zidane found himself with only the goalkeeper to beat from inside the box on the right, but scuffed his shot wide.

On 78 minutes Ferguson made what was to turn out to be a crucial substitution as United pressed for the equaliser they by now deserved. Sheringham came on for Yorke, only his fourth substitute appearance of the year, and immediately made a difference. Within five minutes the net was bulging. The No 10 picked up a Neville throw and laid the ball to Beckham, who delivered a long cross-field pass to Giggs on the far side of the box. Giggs gently volleyed into the box, Cole, unable to get a shot in, laid the ball back, spotting a late run from the United skipper. Keane hit it with all the power he could muster and Sheringham, showing incredibly quick reactions,

Now you know...
Juventus started wearing black and white stripes in 1903 after a member of the club came back from a trip to England with a set of Notts County shirts

diverted it with a diving header past Peruzzi. United's dissent was as sour as their celebrations had been wild when the linesman raised a late, late flag to disallow the goal for offside.

The cavalry charge was at full pelt now as 90 minutes approached and United needed a goal to survive in the tie. It was all long ball from the back, old-fashioned Wimbledon style. Running on to one howitzer from Gary Neville, Giggs put in a quick cross which Cole headed on. Scholes found himself with a free header on the edge of the six-yard box – he hit it straight at the keeper. Another thumping ball from Neville found Giggs on the left, another fine cross from the Welshman saw Scholes then Sheringham have goal-bound shots saved by adrenaline-fuelled Italian legs.

The fourth official's board was hoisted up to show three minutes of extra time. Cole ran at Peruzzi, pushed the ball past him, and seemed to get body-checked by the Italian keeper. No penalty. Then an incredible scramble in the Juventus box after a long throw by Neville was only partially headed away by Ferrara. Zidane, attempting a hooked clearance, managed just

to send the ball back into Juventus' box. Beckham, his back to goal, picked up another loose Italian clearance and cleverly hooked it over his shoulder from the byline. The move, and the match, might have been over had Sheringham not beaten Peruzzi and Iuliano to the ball on the near post, and flicked it across goal. Ferrara got a desperate head to the ball to prevent Cole charging in, but Giggs was lurking and he emphatically half-volleyed the ball into the roof of the net. United's joy was unconfined – they had fashioned themselves a lifeline in the second leg, and their European Cup dream was still alive, if hanging by a thread.

> ❝ It was a fantastic game of football with no nastiness, no cheating. The referee was excellent and we must hope we get one that good in Turin ❞
>
> ALEX FERGUSON

MANCHESTER UNITED					1
HOME TEAM	GOALS mins	ASSISTS mins	SHOTS ON	OFF	SUB'D mins
1 PETER SCHMEICHEL					
2 GARY NEVILLE					
3 DENIS IRWIN					
21 HENNING BERG					45
6 JAAP STAM					
16 ROY KEANE			1	1	
18 PAUL SCHOLES			1	3	
7 DAVID BECKHAM			1		
11 RYAN GIGGS	90		2		
9 ANDREW COLE			4		
19 DWIGHT YORKE					78

SUBSTITUTES	GOALS mins	ASSISTS mins	SHOTS ON	OFF	SUB'D for
17 RAI VAN DER GOUW					
5 RONNY JOHNSEN					#21
10 TEDDY SHERINGHAM					#19
12 PHIL NEVILLE					
8 NICKY BUTT					
15 OLE GUNNAR SOLSKJAER					
21 JESPER BLOMQVIST					

MATCH STATS
SHOTS ON TARGET 6 FOULS 20 OFFSIDES 7
SHOTS OFF TARGET 7 FREE KICKS 7 CORNER KICKS 6

UNITED'S RATING 80%

JUVENTUS					1
AWAY TEAM	GOALS mins	ASSISTS mins	SHOTS ON	OFF	SUB'D mins
1 ANGELO PERUZZI					
3 ZORAN MIRKOVIC					
17 GIANLUCA PESSOTTO			1		
13 MARK IULIANO					
4 PAULO MONTERO					68
8 ANTONIO CONTE	25		1		
7 ANGELO DI LIVIO			2		74
14 DIDIER DESCHAMPS			1		
26 EDGAR DAVIDS		25			
21 ZINEDINE ZIDANE			1	2	
9 FILIPPO INZAGHI			2	1	87

SUBSTITUTES	GOALS mins	ASSISTS mins	SHOTS ON	OFF	SUB'D for
2 CIRO FERRARA					#4
20 ALESSIO TACCHINARDI					#7
24 JUAN ESNAIDER					#9
12 MICHELANGELO RAMPULLA					
15 ALEX BIRINDELLI					
19 IGOR TUDOR					
16 NICOLA AMORUSO					

MATCH STATS
SHOTS ON TARGET 10 FOULS 7 OFFSIDES 3
SHOTS OFF TARGET 9 FREE KICKS 20 CORNER KICKS 15

JUVE'S RATING 85%

Real-ly good

Juve's away goal meant that a 0–0 draw or a win in Turin would put them into their fourth consecutive final, a feat not achieved since Real Madrid in the 1950s.

The Italian job

| SEMI-FINAL Second Leg | 17 APRIL 1999 | Stadio Delle Alpi | Att: 79,528 | Ref: U Meier (Switzerland) | Entertainment: 100% |

Juventus 2 Manchester United 3 Juventus: Inzaghi United: Keane, Yorke, Cole

The run-in to the second leg of the semi-final against Juventus in Turin was spiced up by an extraordinary attack on Juventus' playmaker Zinedine Zidane by Gianni Agnelli, owner of both the club and Fiat. Sparked by rumours that the World and European Player of the Year wanted to leave the club because he was homesick and his wife Veronique wanted to live by the seaside, the tycoon fumed, "Zidane is not suffering from homesickness, he is suffering from being under the thumb of his wife. I have asked him who the boss is in his family. He replied that now he has two children it is his wife. I would like him to play here next season but his wife is a problem because I have no power over her."

It was the sort of political unrest, typical of Italian teams, that can't have done much for team morale, which was otherwise high after the previous Sunday's game in which Juventus severely damaged Lazio's chances of winning Serie A by beating them 3–1 in Rome, even with a much-weakened team – Ancelotti had rested a number of key players, including the Frenchman.

In circumstances like these, Alex Ferguson did not need to employ any of his customary kidology, doing his best to gee up his team by instilling in them a belief that they could win. "Now I feel that we are capable of playing against anyone and I have a genuine feeling we will beat Juventus," he said. "We have more control and patience about our game now and hopefully that will carry us through. We know we have to score and if you look at our record away from home in Europe there is plenty of evidence that we can do that." He looked back to historical precedent to strengthen his case. "We were in this situation in the European Cup-Winners' Cup in 1991 against Montpellier when we drew 1–1 at home, and won 2–0 over there. It's a psychological thing and, hopefully, it's in our favour." Montpellier were one thing, however, Juventus quite another.

The United manager's main worry before the game was the fitness or otherwise of his Welsh

Where on Earth?

Turin, in north-west Italy, is an ancient Roman city which now has a population of just over a million.

England expects

The Stadio delle Alpi was the scene of another great semi-final with home interest. It was in the purpose-built Turin stadium that England drew 1–1 with Germany in the semi of Italia 90, only to go out of the competition cruelly on penalties. It was the closest England have come to winning the world's top competition since 1966.

Ice one Giggsy

Catching the first class Turin train . . .

. . . to the Stadio delle Alpi

Time for action

"Where've my subs got to?"

winger Ryan Giggs, who had scored a wonder-goal against Arsenal in the FA Cup semi-final the previous Wednesday – and left the game on crutches. The No 11 looked doubtful for Turin, and perhaps it was with this in mind that Juve manager Carlo Ancelotti stated, of Giggs, "Without doubt he is United's best player and we are worried about him. He is dangerous in any situation and as we saw the other day he can turn a game in seconds."

Other Juventus stars were surprisingly fulsome in their praise for United. Zinedine Zidane said of Ferguson, "He has produced a team which is least British in style. So much of your game is physical but United have a strong element of creativity and fantasy and that makes them different. He has also kept the great British strengths and that is what explains their success." Didier Deschamps, meanwhile, being either extremely frank or extremely crafty, offered his suggestion as to who

Ferguson should play up front. "The problem for Yorke and Cole is that they play like Italians and therefore present the same challenge with which our defence are presented every week in Serie A. Sheringham is very dangerous. He is the type of player we do not face regularly, and when we do, we always find it difficult."

If all this was a cunning ploy to give United a false sense of security, Edgar Davids put a stick in the spokes with a vicious attack on the midfield. "United are supposed to have the best midfield in Europe," ranted the contentious gangsta-rap lover. "Well I didn't see too much of them at Old Trafford. We were like a steam train overrunning them. But the longer I was out there, looking at opponents who had been described as such big stars, the more I realised what was in it for us. I have no fears of them any more."

What was clear in the minds of the managers of both clubs was that Juventus would start the

A winger and a prayer

game at a furious pace, despite the fact that a 0–0 draw would get them through. "We should start the game as if it was 0–0," stated Ancelotti. "We will attack from the start. That is our only option. It will be very hard because of United's strength, but we also have the strength and determination to get the result we need."

Ferguson agreed with the sentiment, if not the final outcome. "Knowing Juventus they will try to finish the tie in the first half hour, because that is the sort of side they are. The important thing for us is to remember that if we score over there that can change the whole thing."

Another thing was clear at the outset of the game: United needed to score to get through, and probably to win the tie. Looking back in history, it would not be an easy task. In 41 years of European football, Juventus had only been beaten in Turin on seven occasions, and United had never beaten an Italian side away from home. Everything was set for a tough game.

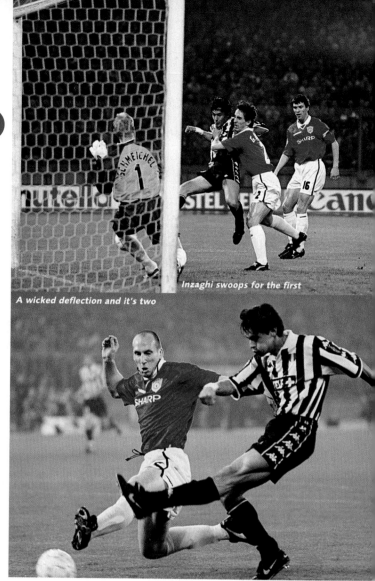

Now you know...
Juventus beat Liverpool 1–0 in 1985, in a European
Cup Final overshadowed by the deaths of 39 Italians

Inzaghi swoops for the first

A wicked deflection and it's two

On the night Giggs, although on the mend, couldn't make it and Blomqvist took his place on the left. Ferguson opted to keep his Yorke-Cole strike partnership up front and, rather surprisingly, decided to drop Scholes in favour of Butt, presumably to firm up the midfield. Juve had hardman Paolo Montero starting on the bench with even-harder-man Ferrara replacing him as a starter and Birindelli on the right in place of Mirkovic.

The teams kicked off in a fog of smoke from the Juventus fans' flares – the 64,500-capacity stadium was full for the first time in the season. After a cat-and-mouse start Juventus made the first break, when a Zinedine Zidane pass found Inzaghi, who chested into the box, challenging Jaap Stam to a race. Stam turned up the pace, got to the ball first, and cleared it into touch: 1–0 to the Dutchman in their own private duel.

Pretty soon, however, and back in the real game, it was 1–0 to Juventus. Beckham made a recovering tackle but gave away a corner in the process. United allowed Zidane to play it short to Di Livio, receive the return and better the angle on his cross, which sailed over everybody before finally finding Inzaghi, who had managed to get in front of Gary Neville but still had the defender hanging on his back, on the far post. The Italian was sharp and strong enough to stick out a leg. 1–0 and Juventus had the best possible of starts. Or so they thought.

United were stunned, but not into inactivity. After some neat midfield passing Keane lobbed a ball into the box to Neville who had run behind his marker. The right back hit a looping, first-time cross that fell perfectly for Cole who, waiting on the edge of the six-yard box, tried an athletic overhead kick. Either side of Peruzzi and United would have been level. Unfortunately the ball went straight at the keeper who held well.

On 11 minutes Juventus fought back, getting the ball out wide to Pessotto on the left after Blomqvist had been dispossessed. Pessotto laid the ball into the now familiar channel, with Inzaghi and Stam again racing down the left side of the box for possession. This time Inzaghi found room for a shot, Stam stretched a leg out to block it and the ball looped

agonisingly millimetres over a static Schmeichel's fingertips and into the goal. The fog hadn't yet cleared from the first goal, and unbelievably Juventus were 2–0 up on the night, 3–1 on aggregate. United had a particularly large mountain to climb.

Many sides would have lost heart at that point and been subjected to a humiliating thrashing. United carried on playing, sometimes to cavalier extremes, still maintaining the belief they could get something out of the night. One way to by-pass the industrious Italian midfield was to lob the ball over their heads, and on 21 minutes Schmeichel did that and Butt backheaded the ball into Yorke's path. It was a route-one move, but effective nonetheless, and Yorke beat one defender before dribbling into the area and shaping to shoot. But Ferrara grabbed the collar of his shirt from behind like a school teacher stopping an unruly kid and Yorke fell in the box. It was surely a penalty, or

Spooky...
Juventus had not lost a European Cup tie over two legs since 5 November 1986 – exactly the same day that Alex Ferguson was appointed manager of Manchester United.

> **"Suddenly we were pushed back into our area and they won a corner. From then on everything went wrong for us"**
>
> FILIPPO INZAGHI

Keane heads United back into the game . . .

. . . and heads back to the half-way line

at least a free kick in Beckham-zone but there was no whistle from Swiss referee Meier. When the ball broke loose Beckham attempted a shot from just outside the box, which was blocked – by Ferrara's hand. The referee whistled this time, but only to award a free kick to Juventus for offside.

Within three minutes Ferrara gave away a corner from a Cole cross, and justice was done. Beckham angled in the kick, and a late run by Keane saw the Irishman rise above three defenders and the goalkeeper, risking a high-speed head butt from Zidane and a thump in the face from Peruzzi, to glance a header powerfully into the net. United were back in the game thanks to a real captain's goal – his fifth of the season, third in Europe. The score was now 2–1 on the night, 3–2 on aggregate, and United knew that another goal, due to the away-goals-counting-double rule, would put them in the driving seat.

Ferguson's men were now playing with much more self-belief and Cole managed to divert another long ball from Irwin into the path of Yorke, but the Tobagan blasted his shot well wide from outside the box. The Reds were pouring forward, but leaving holes at the back in their efforts to equalise and Juventus knew that a further goal for them would virtually put them out of sight. Zidane's run down the left wing ended in a cross which found Conte in the middle of the penalty box. Schmeichel had come for the cross, got nowhere near it and the Juve skipper looped his header over the Dane and towards the goal. Stam, however, read the situation perfectly, running back to the goal-line and stooping to calmly head the ball away for a corner while Inzaghi looked on when he might well have knocked the ball in himself.

Three minutes later calamity struck for United. Blomqvist played a simple midfield ball to Keane who let it run too far, and realising that Zidane was in a position to dispossess him, went in with a wild tackle. Zidane flew into the air and the referee produced a yellow card. It meant that even if Keane managed to lead United to the final, he would be ineligible to play in it.

The chances of that happening dramatically increased after United's next attack on 34 minutes. Another long ball from Neville again eliminated the Juve midfield and Cole, on the edge of the box, controlled it and ran down the right-hand side. Seeing his strike partner Yorke making a run down the middle, he looped in a cross and Yorke found a yard of space on Ferrara by diving horizontally at the ball, heading it past Peruzzi and into the net, getting up with a smile even broader than usual to be engulfed in joyful team-mates. It was his eighth European goal of the season but his first of any kind for six weeks. United were level but they had scored that all-important extra away goal

Calamity for Keano

The Butt stops here for Zidane

and now it was Juventus who needed another.

The Italians, despite a shot on the turn by Inzaghi from the same position he had scored his second goal, didn't respond to United's brace of goals in the same way United had responded to theirs, and United very nearly made it 3-2 before the break. Another long ball by Gary Neville (what's wrong with Wimbledon tactics when you've got class players to employ them?) was headed away by Iuliano to Dwight Yorke, who controlled it and beat a defender with his first touch and cracked in a shot with his second. The ball hit the inside of the post, with Blomqvist just unable to profit from the rebound. When the half-time whistle sounded it was the Juventus players, all bowed heads and misplaced passes, who were happy to hear it. Oh, and the fans, who

It's Yorke, it's 2-2!

Becks earns his stripes

needed a moment or two to catch their breath.

Ancelotti, inevitably, made changes at half time, straight-swapping centre halves Montero and Iuliano and replacing right back Birindelli with centre-forward Amoruso. Di Livio was moved to right back, and Zidane to midfield, leaving the Italians with a classic British-style 4-4-2 system (though United could bet their bottom lira that Di Livio and Pessotto would attack down the wings). True enough, within minutes Zidane found Pessotto on the left, who in turn laid the ball into Inzaghi, once again one on one with Stam. Again the No 9 got his shot in; this time Schmeichel saved with his feet.

The stadium was strangely quiet as Juventus started, for the first time since the opening salvoes, to take over the game. Though this time they were rarely finding a final ball to trouble the United defence. United, for their part, were happy to concede the majority of possession and attack on the break; another long Gary Neville ball from defence was flicked on by Yorke to Beckham on the right; his precise low cross found Cole ahead of his marker on the penalty spot. For once, however, the United striker's control let him down and his half-control half-shot with his right foot flashed harmlessly past the post. Another break soon after saw United win a corner which Yorke, positioned to score, headed into the hands of Peruzzi.

Juventus were bound to create chances of their own, however, and on 61 minutes they had the ball in the net. Stam headed a Di Livio ball out of the box, but Blomqvist couldn't pick it up and Conte slid in to put the ball into

66 The first 45 minutes were the best Manchester United have played in my time at the club 99

ALEX FERGUSON

Inzaghi's path with Schmeichel committed on his near post. The Italian international walked the ball into the net, though you could tell from his muted celebrations that he knew in his heart of hearts he had been at least a yard offside and there were no complaints when the referee disallowed the goal for that reason.

It was United's turn to take over the game. Blomqvist's substitution by Scholes gave the Reds more fluidity in midfield, and a beautiful movement that involved fully 13 United passes saw the redhead find Irwin charging in space on the left. The Irishman dribbled into the box, worked his way past Di Livio and found space for a shot which he hit across the keeper... and onto the inside of the post.

United were still not out of the woods, and their path was made more difficult by the referee and his bizarre yellow-card policy. The Swiss official saw fit to ignore the fact that Ferrara had palmed Cole in the face then waved a card at Scholes for protesting that his two-footed tackle on Deschamps, who himself had gone over the top, was a foul. It was a personal tragedy for the United No 18 who realised that should United make it to the final, he would be joining Keane as no more than a spectator.

United won another corner and while Beckham was waiting to take it Juventus brought Uruguayan attacker Fonseca on for Di Livio. Although breaking a golden rule of management it was to prove a providential switch, for it was the South American who

66 I'm gutted for them both [Keane and Scholes] – it's heartbreak, absolutely tragic 99

ALEX FERGUSON

Is it a penalty?

No, it's a goal

saved Yorke's subsequent header off the line, with Peruzzi well-beaten. Inzaghi reminded United that the Italians needed to score with a close chance, but that was more than matched by Cole, who shot over after a slick United movement involving 20 passes. Olé!

United had proved that they could mix short passing with a long-ball game, and it was more route-one tactics that sealed the game for them. Montero, deep in Juve territory, was unable to control Schmeichel's huge punt and Yorke picked up the rebound. Faced by a potential Ferrara and Montero sandwich he played the ball between the two of them and ran through into the box, making the most of a fortuitous rebound. One-on-one with the keeper, he coolly opted to jink past to the right instead of shooting and Peruzzi's frenzied dive at his feet brought him down. The referee, seeing that Cole was backing up, refrained from blowing his whistle and the No 9 put the ball in from a narrow angle. 3–2 with six minutes left and Juventus now needed two goals to win through.

The Italians were spent men, however, and, with the Stadio Delle Alpi echoing to the very English refrain of "We shall not be moved" from the 6,000 English fans, United created the last good chance of the game. Irwin, proving there's life after Giggs on the left, put in an inch-perfect cross for Beckham, for once in the centre, who belted a volley from the edge of the box... just wide of the post. It was to prove the last significant action of the game and United, despite all the odds, were in the final of the European Cup for the first time since 1968.

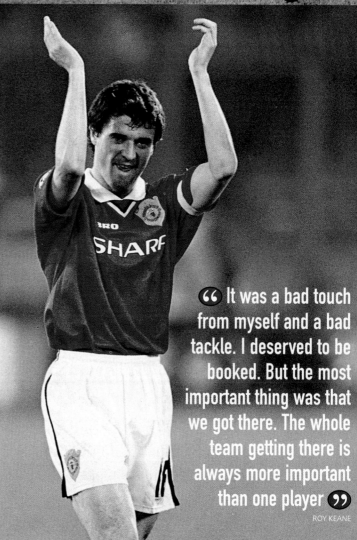

66 It was a bad touch from myself and a bad tackle. I deserved to be booked. But the most important thing was that we got there. The whole team getting there is always more important than one player 99

ROY KEANE

You'll Neville walk alone

> 66 We were the better team tonight. We played with great tempo and rhythm and they found it hard to get the ball from us, particularly in the first half 99
>
> ALEX FERGUSON

JUVENTUS · 2

HOME TEAM		GOALS mins	ASSISTS mins	SHOTS ON OFF	SUB'D mins
1	ANGELO PERUZZI				
2	CIRO FERRARA				
17	GIANLUCA PESSOTTO		10		
13	MARK IULIANO				45
15	ALESSANDRO BIRINDELLI				45
8	ANTONIO CONTE				
7	ANGELO DI LIVIO				80
14	DIDIER DESCHAMPS				
26	EDGAR DAVIDS				
21	ZINEDINE ZIDANE		6		
9	FILIPPO INZAGHI	6, 10		4	1

SUBSTITUTES		GOALS mins	ASSISTS mins	SHOTS ON OFF	SUB'D for
4	PAULO MONTERO				#13
16	NICOLA AMORUSO				#15
11	DANIEL FONSECA				#7
24	JUAN ESNAIDER				
12	MICHEL RAMPULLA				
20	ALESSIO TACCHINARDI				
19	IGOR TUDOR				

MATCH STATS
SHOTS ON TARGET 4 FOULS 10 OFFSIDES 6
SHOTS OFF TARGET 1 FREE KICKS 19 CORNER KICKS 3

JUVE'S RATING 73%

MANCHESTER UNITED · 3

HOME TEAM		GOALS mins	ASSISTS mins	SHOTS ON OFF	SUB'D mins
1	PETER SCHMEICHEL				
2	GARY NEVILLE				
3	DENIS IRWIN			1	
21	RONNY JOHNSEN				
6	JAAP STAM				
7	DAVID BECKHAM		24	1	
8	NICKY BUTT			1	
16	ROY KEANE	24		1	
15	JESPER BLOMQVIST				68
9	ANDREW COLE	84	34	4	
19	DWIGHT YORKE	34	84	2 3	

SUBSTITUTES		GOALS mins	ASSISTS mins	SHOTS ON OFF	SUB'D for
17	RAI VAN DER GOUW				
12	PHIL NEVILLE				
18	PAUL SCHOLES				#15
10	TEDDY SHERINGHAM				
20	OLE GUNNAR SOLSKJAER				
24	WES BROWN				

MATCH STATS
SHOTS ON TARGET 7 FOULS 19 OFFSIDES 5
SHOTS OFF TARGET 6 FREE KICKS 10 CORNER KICKS 4

UNITED'S RATING 90%

Pasta sell-by date

United knocking Juventus out of the competition ended an incredible run of seven consecutive years with an Italian team in the final of the European Cup – no English teams had reached such heights since Liverpool back in 1985.

> 66 Funnily enough our two-goal lead worked to their advantage. It gave us the impression it would be easy and we stepped back and didn't play aggressively enough 99
>
> JUVENTUS COACH CARLO ANCELOTTI

“ I hope my greatest night is still to come ”

ALEX FERGUSON

Now you know...
Bayern beat Atletico Madrid 4–0 in 1974, the only time the European Cup Final went to a replay

Kickin' Kiev

7 April 1999 Semi-final first leg
Dynamo Kiev 3 Bayern Munich 3

Olimpiski Stadium, Kiev

Referee: K Nielsen (Denmark)

Dynamo Kiev were the form team in the tournament and though they were the bookies' outsiders to win the European Cup, very few of the 80,000 fans who packed into the Olimpiski Stadium doubted that their side had the capability of becoming the first Eastern European team to reach the final since Red Star Belgrade in 1991.

Standing in their way were Bayern Munich. The Germans had reached the semis by beating neighbours Kaiserslautern after topping United's Group D, and they were also unbeaten in all competitions for five months.

It was Kiev (who had knocked Arsenal out of the competition) who drew first blood through the irrepressible Andrei Shevchenko, with his seventh goal in the tournament. It was reported early in the season that Shevchenko would move to Milan as soon as Kiev were out of the Champions' League. Well he obviously hadn't wanted to go to Italy during 1998/99 because it was almost entirely thanks to his goals, and his partnership with co-striker Rebrov, that Kiev had got this far.

Shevchenko was the ideal spearhead for Kiev's counter-attacking tactics, and it was a goal on the break that broke the deadlock. Valiantsin Bialkevich's long pass evaded Markus Babbel and Shevchenko was in his favoured position – bearing down on goal, one-on-one with the keeper. Kahn had no chance and within 17 minutes, Kiev were 1–0 up. The home side kept up the pressure and it was Oliver Kahn in the Germans' goal who was responsible for keeping the score down with a couple of great saves, until he came up against Shevchenko again on 43 minutes. This time it was a beautifully curled free kick from the edge of the box, after Thomas Strunz had fouled Vitalei Kossovskyi, and it should have seen Kiev go into the dressing room with a 2–0 lead and huge applause ringing in their ears.

Instead, the crowd were silenced by the Germans who, as is their wont, knocked one in seconds before the whistle. It was Bayern's turn to be awarded a free kick, though at 35-yards out, it didn't look too dangerous. Not until Michael Tarnat belted the ball past the stunned keeper Shovkovski, that is.

Kiev went on the attack as the match resumed after half time and might well have had a goal within a minute had Andrei Husin managed to keep his header on target instead of putting it wide after Rebrov's cross from the byline. But it didn't take long. Vitalei Kossovskyi attempted to pass into the penalty area, Samuel Kuffour tried to clear but could only hit the ball straight

Kuffour and Shevchenko battle it out for a place in the final

Kiev and Bayern, like Jeremies and Shevchenko, neck and neck

back to him, and the forward gleefully thumped home from ten yards. The match was perfectly poised at 3–1; a goal for the Ukranians would put them virtually out of sight, while a second away goal from the Germans would give them a distinct psychological advantage in the second leg.

In the end, on a heavy pitch, it was Kiev who, tired by their relentless pace, were forced onto the back foot. On the 78th minute Effenberg perfectly flighted a free kick in off the post and the Germans sniffed a famous comeback. Kiev recovered and had several chances to make the score 4–2, including a Matthaus clearance off the line and a Shevchenko free kick deflected for a corner. Then, right at the death, Carsten Jancker picked up a loose ball in the area and thumped it past the desolate Shovkovski to equalise and silence the crowd. Now Kiev would need to win in Munich, or fight their way to an unlikely 4–4 draw, to make it through to the final.

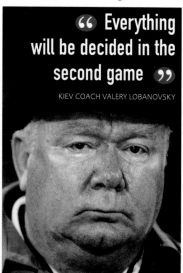

❝ Everything will be decided in the second game ❞

KIEV COACH VALERY LOBANOVSKY

DYNAMO KIEV		**3**
HOME TEAM	GOALS mins	SUB'D mins
1 OLEX SHOVKOVSKI		
2 OLEH LUZHNYI		
4 OLEX HOLOVKO		
5 VLADYSLAV VASCHUK		
7 KAKHA KALADZE		
9 VITALEI KOSSOVSKYI	50	
10 ANDREI SHEVCHENKO	16, 43	
11 SERGI REBROV		
14 ANDREI HUSIN		
15 ALEX KHATSKEVICH		81
24 VALIANTSIN BIALKEVICH		

SUBSTITUTES	GOALS mins	SUB'D for
12 VIACH KERNOZENKO		
3 ALEXEI GUERASSIMENKO		
17 SERGI FEDOROV		
22 SERGI KONOVALOV		
23 OLEX KIRIUKHIN		#15
30 ARTEM YASHKIN		
31 SERGI KORMILTSEV		

BAYERN MUNICH		**3**
AWAY TEAM	GOALS mins	SUB'D mins
1 OLIVER KAHN		
2 MARKUS BABBEL		
4 SAMUEL KUFFOUR		
7 MEHMET SCHOLL		72
8 THOMAS STRUNZ		
10 LOTHAR MATTHAUS		
11 STEFAN EFFENBERG	78	
16 JENS JEREMIES		
18 MICHAEL TARNAT	45	
19 CARSTEN JANCKER	88	90
20 HASAN SALIHAMIDZIC		

SUBSTITUTES	GOALS mins	SUB'D for
22 BERND DREHER		
5 THOMAS HELMER		
28 THORSTEN FINK		
21 ALEXANDER ZICKLER		#7
24 ALI DAEI		#19
25 THOMAS LINKE		

Bayern Barça bound

Luton reject

21 April 1999 Semi-final 2nd leg
Bayern Munich 1 Dynamo Kiev 0

Olimpiastadion, Munich
Referee: V Melo Pereira (Portugal)

Needing to win, Dynamo Kiev naturally started their match in Munich on the attack, forcing Bayern keeper Oliver Kahn to make a string of brilliant saves in the opening minutes to keep his team on level terms in front of a sell-out 60,000 crowd in the Olympic stadium in Munich. In the first minute, the blond Schmeichel-lookalike palmed away a 35-yard blaster from Alex Khatskevich then reacted brilliantly minutes later to save at the feet of Valiantsin Bialkevich.

Bayern, however, gradually wrested control of the match and scored a vital goal on 35 minutes to virtually seal their passage to Barcelona. Lothar Matthaus picked up a clearance from a corner and tapped the ball to Mario Basler, Bayern's erratic smoking, drinking wunderboy.

Supermario, as he is dubbed on his better days by the Bayern fans, went past three defenders before curling the

ball in off the far post from outside the box. A fantastic goal from a player, who, only days earlier had stated he was out of love with the game, and had been persuaded to

❝ Oliver Kahn has shown tonight he is one of the best in the world ❞

OTTO HITZFELD

play to his full potential by Otto Hitzfeld. "I'm pleased for him," said Hitzfeld after the game. "He's had a difficult time but he scored a dream goal."

Sergi Rebrov could have equalised for the Ukranians before half time, but another brilliant save from Oliver Kahn denied him. When play kicked off in the second half, Bayern continued their dominance but chance after chance went begging. Carsten 'The Tank' Jancker hit a superb volley over the bar in the 66th minute and Iranian striker Ali Daei, just on as sub, hit a header wide on 77 minutes.

After the game, manager Otto Hitzfeld said, "I am happy to see Manchester United again. We had two very exciting group matches, especially the second in Manchester. The crowd in Barcelona will see two teams who play attractive football and they can enjoy it. And may the best team win!"

BAYERN MUNICH		1
AWAY TEAM	GOALS mins	SUB'D mins
1 OLIVER KAHN		
2 MARKUS BABBEL		
4 SAMUEL KUFFOUR		
10 LOTHAR MATTHAUS		
11 STEFAN EFFENBERG		
14 MARIO BASLER	35	
16 JENS JEREMIES		
18 MICHAEL TARNAT		84
19 CARSTEN JANCKER		75
21 ALEXANDER ZICKLER		75
25 THOMAS LINKE		

SUBSTITUTES	GOALS mins	SUB'D for
12 SVEN SCHUER		
5 THOMAS HELMER		
7 MEHMET SCHOLL		
8 THOMAS STRUNZ		
28 THORSTEN FINK		#18
20 HASAN SALIHAMIDZIC		#21
24 ALI DAEI		#19

DYNAMO KIEV		0
AWAY TEAM	GOALS mins	SUB'D mins
1 OLEX SHOVKOVSKI		
2 OLEH LUZHNYI		
4 OLEX HOLOVKO		
5 VLADYSLAV VASCHUK		
7 KAKHA KALADZE		
9 VITALEI KOSSOVSKYI		
10 ANDREI SHEVCHENKO		
11 SERGI REBROV		
14 ANDREI HUSIN		82
15 ALEX KHATSKEVICH		
24 VALIANTSIN BIALKEVICH		

SUBSTITUTES	GOALS mins	SUB'D for
12 VIACH KERNOZENKO		
18 VASSYL KARDASH		#14
22 SERGI KONOVALOV		
23 OLEX KIRIUKHIN		
30 ARTEM YASHKIN		
31 SERGI KORMILTSEV		
32 VOLODYMYR YEZERSKYI		

" We haven't won anything yet, but this could be a great year for us. This team has great potential "

FRANZ BECKENBAUER

Bayern on track for the final

Unbelievable...

United's last-gasp heroes

Ninety minutes are up...

| CHAMPIONS' LEAGUE FINAL | 26 May 1999 | Nou Camp, Barcelona | Att: 90,000 | Ref: P Collina (Italy) | Entertainment: 100% |

Manchester United 2 Bayern Munich 1 United: Sheringham, Solskjaer Bayern: Basler

An estimated sixty thousand United fans travelled to Barcelona any which way they could, half of them without tickets, many of them looking forward to the first European Cup Final for their club in their lifetime. They slept where they could – the city's hotels were sold out days before the game and the police found more than a few tired revellers attempting to sleep on the five-kilometre beach that lies between the beautiful, bustling city and the sea. The players, meanwhile, arrived in the Mediterranean port in rather more style, on Concorde, and immediately transferred to their luxury hotel in the trendy resort of Sitges, a few miles south of the Catalan capital. Their worries were more whether they'd get in the team than into the stadium.

For the thirty thousand or so ticketless Reds life was difficult in the run-up to the game. Touts were selling tickets for up to £1,000 each; a sum which a few stumped up for some clever forgeries – spottable by the unfortunate spelling mistake (*Grandaria* instead of *Gradaria*). One unfortunate fan (named by the police as Michael R) gave a Spanish tout 7.1 million pesetas (£28,000) on the understanding that the guy would turn up the next day with 116 tickets. Unsurprisingly, he didn't show.

Barcelona was full, too, of countless German fans, who added to the carnival atmosphere of the city in the days before the game. Bayern, like United, were on course for a historic treble, having already won their league at a canter and with a place in the German Cup final two weeks on. Indeed, the similarities between the clubs were striking. Both teams had dominated their domestic scene in recent years (Bayern had won 14 titles in 30 years). Both teams had qualified to the Champions' League as runners-up (this was to be the first European Cup Final not to have been won by a national or European champion). Both teams were supported by fans all over their respective countries (the average journey distance for Bayern's fans at home games is 62 miles). Neither club had won Europe's premier trophy for years (United's only triumph coming in '68, Bayern's last win back in 1976). But the main difference between the clubs was that United

England v Germany

West Ham 2–0 1860 Munich
(1965 Cup-Winners' Cup)
Dortmund 2–1 Liverpool
(1966 Cup-Winners' Cup)
Liverpool 3–0 Borussia Mönchengladbach
(1973 UEFA Cup)
Bayern 2–0 Leeds
(1975 European Cup)
Liverpool 3–1 Borussia Mönchengladbach
(1977 European Cup)
Aston Villa 1–0 Bayern
(1982 European Cup)
Chelsea 1–0 Stuttgart
(1998 Cup-Winners' Cup)
Man United 2–1 Bayern
(1999 European Cup)

Total England 6 Germany 2

Captain Fergie guides the team to Barcelona . . . again

The outsider

The Opposition (1)

Stefan Effenberg, 31, the complete midfielder. With a penchant for unexpected passes and explosive free kicks, the slick Effenberg has twice refused to ever play again for Germany. Brought to the club pre-season, he has added a much-needed touch of class to the team.

were on the stock market whereas Bayern were owned by their 80,000 members, and run by a six-man *praesidium* including former players and German legends Uli Hoeness, Franz Beckenbauer and Karl-Heinz Rummenigge.

The managers played the waiting game very differently, Otto Hitzfeld revealing his team on Monday, Alex Ferguson keeping his under wraps until Wednesday, though giving a few hints to the press the day before. Hitzfeld, without the injured Giovane Elber and Bixente Lizarazu, opted for his normal 3-4-1-2 tactics, with Kahn in goal, Matthaus as sweeper, Kuffour and Linke in central defence, Tarnat and Babbel as wing backs, Jeremies and Effenberg in central midfield and Jancker and Zickler up front with Mario Basler playing the all-important role in the hole behind the strikers.

Effenberg was cited as the key player in the team. The volatile midfielder, bought by Hitzfeld in the summer despite pressure from above not to, in his second spell at the club, was perhaps the most unpopular player in Germany, earning the nickname 'Stinkfinger' after making an obscene gesture to fans at USA 94 on being substituted. But he had added much-needed flair to Bayern's midfield and had helped turn them from also-rans in the Bundesliga (second to unfashionable Kaiserslautern in 1997/98) to European Cup finalists and potential treble winners. Clearly he was the man to watch out for in the German team. "Effenberg is the head of the team, the heart of the team and the brain of the team," cooed Bayern midfielder Mehmet Scholl, while his manager said, "Zidane was the best player in the world this time last year and Effenberg is this year. He is technically perfect and in some situations he can pass like nobody else."

The main debate about the United team sheet in the run-in to the final was about who, with Scholes and Keane suspended, would sit alongside Nicky Butt in the centre of United's

66 Zidane was the best player in the world this time last year and Effenberg is this year 99

BAYERN BOSS OTTO HITZFELD

midfield. At first Ronny Johnsen looked the best bet, a defensive option who would try to nullify the creative talents of Effenberg. Other options included Phil Neville, in a similar role, or Ryan Giggs, who had been promising on a couple of occasions in the centre. Not many expected Ferguson's final decision, hinted at the evening before the game, to play David Beckham in the middle, move Giggs to the right wing and play Jesper Blomqvist on the left. Beckham had shone in the centre in the FA Cup Final the preceding Saturday after the manager had been forced to reshuffle his pack due to Keane's early injury.

Jaap Stam had done enough in the 13 minutes he had played against Newcastle to suggest that his Achilles injury would hold up for one more match, and he was United's defensive lynchpin, with Johnsen chosen instead of the unlucky David May to play in the centre of defence. Irwin, who had missed the FA Cup Final through suspension, and Gary Neville

Becks and Giggsy discuss match tactics and ice-packs, while Keano ponders what might have been

66 I heard Gary Lineker say football was a very simple game — 22 players run after a ball and in the end the Germans win 99

BAYERN SKIPPER LOTHAR MATTHAUS

were the obvious choices to defend United's flanks. One further bone of contention was whether Teddy Sheringham, who had scored and been awarded the man of the match award in the FA Cup, should start up front in place of either Cole or Yorke. Again, though, Ferguson opted for his tried and tested formula, and kept United's normal strike partnership intact.

There was a late injury scare to flutter United supporters' hearts when David Beckham was seen with an ice pack on his thigh at the end of United's training session at the Nou Camp on the eve of the Final. Two key midfielders out would have been bad enough, but three... It turned out that the ice-pack was merely a precaution. Fergie ran the training session in a replica 1968 United top in order to try to rally his troops, and, as if the pressure wasn't already enough before his biggest game, The *Sun* ran a story suggesting that he would be knighted if United won the match. In his final, pre-match press conference Ferguson tried his best to avoid comparisons being made between this team and the boys of '68, and similar

comparisons between himself and Sir Matt Busby. He preferred to talk football, stating that the key to United's success lay in their attack. "Of course we are going to miss a player of Roy Keane's influence," he said of his ineligible captain. "But we know we've also still got the main aces – goalscorers."

Lothar Matthaus, meanwhile, in another conference in another part of the city, was rather more humorous in his appraisal of the match to come. "I heard Gary Lineker say football was a very simple game," he joked. "Twenty-two players run after a ball and in the end the Germans win."

When the inflatable modernist cathedrals had been cleared after a bizarre opening ceremony in the Nou Camp the two teams marched on to the pitch for the 44th European Cup Final to a wall of sound and a mosaic of cards produced by the Bayern fans proclaiming the name of their team. There wasn't, of course, a free seat anywhere in the 90,000-seater stadium, and

The Opposition (2)
Lothar Matthaus, 38, sweeper. Bayern's legendary talisman had recently made the successful conversion to sweeper after losing the pace necessary to play in midfield. As imposing a presence off the field as on it, Matthaus had been at the heart of many of the club's recent internal problems, notably an in-print argument with Jurgen Klinsmann, until calmed down by manager Otto Hitzfeld.

Suits you sir

Now you know...
The only other European Cup Final in Barcelona was in 1989, a Ruud Gullit-inspired Milan thrashed Steaua Bucharest 4-0

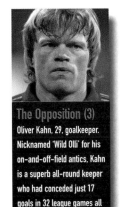

The Opposition (3)
Oliver Kahn, 29, goalkeeper. Nicknamed 'Wild Olli' for his on-and-off-field antics, Kahn is a superb all-round keeper who had conceded just 17 goals in 32 league games all season. His unconventional style isn't limited to his save-making: three weeks before the Final he was fined for biting Dortmund striker Heiko Herrlich on the cheek.

many of the neutral places seemed to have been snapped up by United fans, who clearly outnumbered their counterparts.

The 45,000 or so English in the crowd, however, were soon silenced by events on the pitch, if only momentarily. A scrappy opening, in which both keepers got an early touch of the ball and Effenberg hit a Tarnat cross into the side-netting, was concluded with a quick Bayern move which led to a free-kick on the edge of United's box. Jancker and Stam, who were to be welded together all game, challenged in midfield for a deep clearance from Tarnat, which had been badly controlled by Beckham. Stam slid in to connect, knocking Jancker down in the process, but could only divert it into the path of Jens Jeremies. The midfielder found Zickler on the left wing, and Zickler passed the ball straight to Jancker who had picked himself off the ground sooner than Stam and stolen a couple of yards on the

Zickler gets his teeth into a header

The Opposition (4)
Marin Basler, 31, attacking midfielder. Nicknamed SuperMario, Basler is a brilliant but erratic player who nearly gave up the game after 'falling out of love with it' but was talked back into it by Otto Hitzfeld and scored the semi-final winner that ensured Bayern's place in the Final. A drinker and smoker, Basler was so mistrusted by former manager Giovanni Trappatoni that the Italian put a private detective on his trail.

United need another brick in the wall

Dutchman. As the huge striker bore down on goal, Johnsen barged in, knocking him over on the edge of the box. Referee Pierluigi Collina blew his whistle for a kick in a very, very dangerous area.

Schmeichel arranged a five-man wall – Babbel and Jancker, still marked by Stam, joined in on the end as Mario Basler stood over the ball. As the German No 14 ran up to take the kick, Jancker peeled off, taking Stam with him and Babbel started ducking. Basler hit a low curling ball into the gap that had just appeared and the ball was in the back of the net before Schmeichel, badly unsighted, had time to move. It was a brilliantly worked goal, straight off the training ground. Barely five minutes gone and United were 1–0 down, not for the first time in the campaign.

United started dominating possession as the Germans sat back on their lead, but despite some virtuoso moments from Beckham, playing like it was his ball and he didn't want any one else to play with it, they were unable to turn this possession into clear-cut chances. Part of this was due to their unaccustomed shape – Giggs isn't as effective on the right and Blomqvist is no Giggs on the left – but most of the credit must go to the German

defenders, who, stuck to their opponents like limpet mines, were enormously quick to snuffle out danger, with blocks and tackles, as soon as it raised its head.

Their midfield wasn't half bad either, especially Mario Basler, billed as playing in the hole, but in fact starting everything he did from a position deep on the right. And if Zickler had been less hasty with a cross from the right by the German No 14 – he shot lamely wide when he might have scored – the Germans could well have been 2–0 up within ten minutes.

A couple of United efforts summed up the frustrating night they were beginning to have. Beckham, receiving a knee-high ball in the centre circle, cleverly flicked it over his shoulder to take out Matthaus (who was playing more in midfield than as sweeper at times) and ran into the Bayern half. He saw Cole belting for the goal and laid a seemingly perfect through ball to the United No 9. Thomas Linke, however, stuck out a foot and the effort came to nothing. On another occasion the ball was bobbling around in the area and Cole might have hit it in but wasn't quick enough and Effenberg instead booted it out. The Germans, in fact, looked quicker to anything that came their way in the final third of the field.

Bayern, to make matters worse, looked more dangerous on the break than United did in possession. Schmeichel saved a Zickler diving

Tor!

header and Basler casually hit a free kick over the bar. On several occasions, Jancker was caught up for offside when he didn't look it after going on intelligent runs which made United's back four look very square indeed. The big Jaap Stam lookalike was giving the Dutchman more problems than he was used to – Jancker at times seemed like Jaap's older brother who was both bigger and better than him. Alex Ferguson, on the sidelines, looked a forlorn figure as he realised that his tactical reshuffle was clearly not working.

United didn't manage to fashion a clear chance until the 21st minute. Neville produced a long throw which Yorke hooked towards both the goal and Cole. Kahn bruised in to punch the ball clear. Soon after Beckham found Cole with a lovely ball, but the United striker was unable to make his way through the German wall which immediately appeared in front of him. And again Bayern broke convincingly. Jeremies to Jancker on the edge of the box; Jancker to Zickler with a delicate back flick; Zickler wide from the edge of the box when he might have scored.

Another German attack saw Jeremies bearing down on a loose ball in the United box. Schmeichel got there first, and instead of booting the ball away, he sidestepped the midfielder and went charging up the wing, belting a ball towards Giggs deep in enemy territory. The ball was wide and went off for a throw, but at least the occasion added a rare bit of humour to what was

Now you know...
Lothar Matthaus was also in the side the last time Bayern were in the European Cup Final in 1987 – they lost 2–1 to Porto

becoming an arduous game for the Reds.

Things got slightly better just before the interval. In the last five minutes of the half United finally created a few chances. Yorke found Cole on the edge of the box, Cole dummied the ball and Giggs, who had charged infield from the wing, had a race to the ball with Tarnat by his side and Kahn in front of him. The goalkeeper dived bravely at the Welshman's feet to save. Within two minutes Giggs was on the prowl again and a shot from just outside the box was deflected for a corner. The United No 11 made it a trio of chances when his weak header from a deflected Cole cross was saved by Kahn. The German keeper hadn't yet been stretched by United, but at least they were finding something for him to do.

In the interval, according to Teddy Sheringham afterwards, Alex Ferguson gave a stirring speech to rally his troops. "If you lose, you'll have to go up and get your losers' medals, and you will be six feet away from the European Cup but you will not be able to touch it. And for many of you that will be the closest you will ever get. Don't you dare come back in here without giving your all."

It was Bayern, however, who started the second half in the more positive mood. Jancker bullied his way into the penalty box, rode a tackle from Johnsen and forced a save from Schmeichel from a narrow angle in the first minute. Then Basler tried to catch Schmeichel napping with a snap shot from 30 yards – the Dane proved he was awake by catching the ball. On 53 minutes Basler whipped in an insidious cross from the right – Babbel dived to head it, but, perhaps pulled back by Johnsen, just missed contact. Effenberg collected the ball from the left, hit in another cross, and the diving Kuffour headed wide. United were

Keep your hair on

Referee Pierluigi Collina, a 39-year-old financial consultant with more than a passing resemblance to a thin Uncle Fester, was the first Italian referee to officiate the Final for eight years. The last time was the Red Star Belgrade v Marseilles clash in 1991 and Italian Larese was the whistle blower.

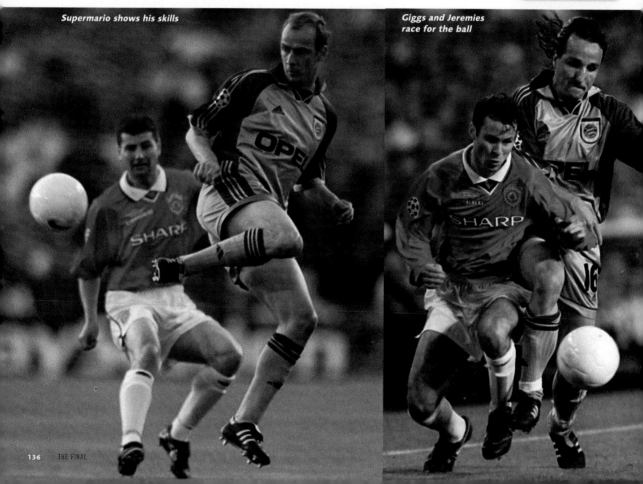

Supermario shows his skills

Giggs and Jeremies race for the ball

Beckham hones his hurdling abilities

finding it so difficult to make chances, Bayern knew that another goal would virtually kill the tie off.

On 63 minutes United created their best move of the match so far. After a long period of possession Giggs put in a left foot cross from the right which found Blomqvist, ahead of his marker, on the edge of the area. The Swede had to stretch to reach the ball, and blasted it over the top. His face said it all afterwards.

The close chance got the fans behind the team again though, and United started perking up. But Bayern were still creating chances and Basler, just inside the United half, very nearly scored with a punt at goal which had the panicky Schmeichel stumbling forlornly backwards. The Dane was happy to see the ball go over the bar.

Ferguson knew he had to change things, and in the 66th minute he substituted Blomqvist for Sheringham. United reformed into a 4-3-3 formation, Giggs moved to the left and Beckham back to the right. It was a gamble, Ferguson was risking Butt being overrun in midfield, but the Scotsman had to do something and after his fine

FA Cup Final appearance the Cockney deserved a chance. United reacted well to the change; Stam headed over from a corner and Cole skewed an overhead kick wide when a solid connection might have created a goal.

Hitzfeld, perhaps sensing that United were gaining the advantage, countered Ferguson's changes with a substitution of his own, bringing on German international midfielder Mehmet Scholl for striker Zickler. And Scholl, who had been plagued with injury all season, immediately made a difference. First he set Effenberg up for a 30-yard blaster which flashed wide of the post, then he found Jancker in the box, enabling the striker to pass across to Effenberg on the left. The Bayern midfielder attempted to volley the ball over Schmeichel – the Dane managed to get his fingertips to it and turn a certain goal into a corner.

On 78 minutes Basler burst down the right flank, hurdled a flying tackle by

Going to the bar

Beckham and belted towards the penalty area. Scholl, who had run in from the other side, took the ball off him on the edge of the box, and with everyone expecting a blasting shot, delicately chipped the ball over Schmeichel's head. The Dane could only turn and watch as the ball looped towards his goal before gratefully catching it as it bounced off the inside of the post and into his welcome arms.

United rallied, Butt played a neat one-two with Yorke on the edge of the box and hit the ball across the goal from the byline. It was too far in front of Cole and went behind Sheringham, however, and the chance, like all of United's so far, came to nothing. There were now just ten minutes left on the clock.

They were to prove highly eventful. Both managers made a further change to their formations – Hitzfeld took off the tiring Matthaus and replaced him with Fink, Ferguson straight-swapped Cole for Solskjaer. And with his first touch of the game the Norwegian forced Kahn into a diving save after getting his head to a fine first-time Gary Neville cross. It was the closest United had come to scoring.

Bayern were to go even closer on two occasions in a spell of pressure that had United fans in despair. First Scholl, with 'olés' ringing in his ears after a brilliant passing movement by the Germans, blasted a shot which Schmeichel fingertipped round the post. Then the substitute headed a clearance from a Basler corner back into the mixer. Jancker, with his back to goal, elegantly bicycle-kicked the ball

on to the United crossbar, just missing the rebound with a comedy resurrection. It was a time in the game when United should have had Bayern pinned into their own half, instead it was them who were on the rack.

Needs will as needs must, however, and United began to fashion some chances of their own as the time ticked by. On 86 minutes Solskjaer fed Sheringham with a neat back-heel, and the United No 10 hit a fierce volley that had Kahn scrambling to save. A minute later Beckham crossed from the right and the ball fell in the path of Dwight Yorke. The Tobagan shaped to half volley the ball into the net but missed it completely in the way you or I might and the ball went through his legs. Giggs thwacked a cross in from the left, Solskjaer got his head to it and Kahn saved.

Although there had been very few stoppages in a highly clean game (Effenberg being the only name in the book after hacking down Giggs) the fourth official raised up a board that spelt hope for United in the shape of the figure three. Three minutes to do what they hadn't managed in the preceding 90 – get the ball past Kahn. They were to prove the most glorious three minutes in the history of the club.

Forty seconds into injury time Beckham made a brave run and fed Neville who hit a cross into the crowded box. Effenberg charged it down. Corner. United's 11th of the game – perhaps, just perhaps, the most important in their history. Schmeichel, who had scored in similar circumstances at Old Trafford against Rotor Volgograd three years before, lumbered up into the box.

There's something unsettling about a goalkeeper in the wrong penalty box, and as Schmeichel rose to meet Beckham's corner he had attracted German defenders like flies to a fallen summer ice cream. The ball went over

the keeper however, ending up on Yorke's head, though the Tobagan could only nod away from goal. Giggs was there on the edge of the box, with a chance to write himself into the history books. He miscued his shot, it fell into Sheringham's path and the United substitute swung a boot at the ball. His connection wasn't clean either but the result was better than he could have hoped. The ball skewed into the corner of the net with Kahn rooted to the goal-line. United, at long last, were level.

Everybody's minds moved onto the gruelling thought of extra time, and perhaps even penalties. With the golden goal-rule operating, after the final whistle the next score, in the manner of park kickabouts, would decide the game. But there was still a minute on the clock, and United gained possession and pumped the ball deep into Bayern territory where Solskjaer was lurking. The Norwegian, with fresher legs than most on the field, headed towards goal and hit in a cross that Kuffour charged down. Another corner.

This time Schmeichel didn't risk coming up, though United did fill the box with bodies.

Yeeeeeeees! We've equalised!

Sheringham heads on . . .

. . .Solskjaer sticks out a boot . . .

. . . and United are in dreamland

Beckham struck an in-swinger, Sheringham, having got away from Linke, headed it across the goal and Solskjaer stuck out a boot to send the ball into the roof of the net, United fans into absolute raptures and anyone with anything to do with Bayern into the sort of deep depression that can last for months. Schmeichel performed a surprisingly graceful cartwheel for such a big man at the other end of the pitch.

The scenes which followed will never be forgotten by anyone who witnessed them. Referee Collina had to pick up several stricken Germans from the ground in order to get them to kick off and play the remaining 13 seconds. When they did restart the game they managed to get the ball into the United box but Butt headed clear and the final whistle sounded. Two minutes before the Germans had been preparing their victory dances. Two minutes on they were despondent. Big Jancker was a broken man, weeping on his knees.

Kuffour, who had given away the final corner of the game and given Ole Solskjaer too much space

The agony and the ecstasy

MANCHESTER UNITED — 2

		GOALS mins	ASSISTS mins	SHOTS ON	SHOTS OFF	SUB'D mins
1	PETER SCHMEICHEL					
2	GARY NEVILLE			1		
3	DENIS IRWIN					
6	JAAP STAM				1	
5	RONNY JOHNSEN				1	
15	JESPER BLOMQVIST				1	67
8	NICKY BUTT					
7	DAVID BECKHAM				1	
11	RYAN GIGGS		90	1		
9	ANDREW COLE				3	81
10	DWIGHT YORKE			1		

SUBSTITUTES		GOALS mins	ASSISTS mins	SHOTS ON	SHOTS OFF	SUB'D for
17	RAI VAN DER GOUW					
20	OLE GUNNAR SOLSKJAER	90		3		#9
12	PHIL NEVILLE			1		
10	TEDDY SHERINGHAM	90	90	1	1	#15
24	WES BROWN					
4	DAVID MAY					
34	JONATHAN GREENING					

MATCH STATS

				UNITED'S RATING
SHOTS ON TARGET 7	FOULS 11	OFFSIDES 5		85%
SHOTS OFF TARGET 7	FREE KICKS 10	CORNER KICKS 11		

BAYERN MUNICH — 1

		GOALS mins	ASSISTS mins	SHOTS ON	SHOTS OFF	SUB'D mins
1	OLIVER KAHN					
25	THOMAS LINKE					
10	LOTHAR MATTHAUS				1	80
4	SAMUEL KUFFOUR				1	
2	MARKUS BABBEL					
18	MICHAEL TARNAT					
16	JENS JEREMIES					
11	STEFAN EFFENBERG			1	1	
14	MARIO BASLER	6		2	3	90
19	CARSTEN JANCKER			1	1	
21	ALEXANDER ZICKLER			1	1	71

SUBSTITUTES		GOALS mins	ASSISTS mins	SHOTS ON	SHOTS OFF	SUB'D for
22	BERND DREHER					
7	MEHMET SCHOLL			1	1	#21
17	THORSTEN FINK					#10
20	HASAN SALIHAMIDZIC					#14
5	THOMAS HELMER					
8	THOMAS STRUNZ					
24	ALI DAEI					

MATCH STATS

				BAYERN'S RATING
SHOTS ON TARGET 6	FOULS 10	OFFSIDES 8		80%
SHOTS OFF TARGET 10	FREE KICKS 11	CORNER KICKS 7		

66 I can't believe it. I can't believe it. Football. Bloody Hell 99 ALEX FERGUSON

when it came in, was bashing his hand on the ground in the manner of a cartoon baddie whose dastardly plans had been thwarted.

For the next ten minutes there was pandemonium on the pitch and in the stands, with an incredibly marked distinction between the jubilant Reds and the despondent Germans. Ferguson hugged each and every one of his players who formed a line and jumped up and down in glee. The Germans remained on the ground. Eventually they wearily rose to receive their losers medals (Matthaus disdainfully took his straight off his neck) and trudged off the pitch to leave the United players to their glory. They crowded onto the space-age podium, kissed the huge trophy, and settled back for the symbolic moment of triumph. Schmeichel, captain for the day, having just played his 397th and final game for the club, and Ferguson, a manager who had finally found the end of the rainbow, lifted the trophy together. Neither of them could have been totally sure that the events that led to them being there had actually happened. But they had. United, in the most dramatic of circumstances, had won the European Cup for the first time since 1968 – and the Treble to boot.

" Having won it, I feel a sense of fulfilment I did not feel before. You look at the Cup and the managers who have lifted it and the teams that have won it recently. There was Ajax, Juventus, Borussia Dortmund, Real Madrid and now Manchester United... Maybe we were meant to win it. Maybe there was an element of destiny **"**

ALEX FERGUSON

Other titles available from Manchester United Books

	0 233 99045 3	Cantona On Cantona by Eric Cantona	£14.99
	0 233 99359 2	Sir Matt Busby: A Tribute by Rick Glanvill	£14.99
	0 233 99047 X	Alex Ferguson: Ten Glorious Years by Jim Drewett and Alex Leith	£9.99
	0 233 99046 1	Ryan Giggs: Genius At Work by Alex Leith	£9.99
	0 233 99362 2	Odd Man Out: A Player's Diary by Brian McClair	£6.99
	0 233 99178 6	Manchester United in the Sixties by Graham McColl	£12.99
	0 233 99368 1	Alex Ferguson: A Will To Win by Alex Ferguson with David Meek	£6.99
	0 233 99453 X	Manchester United Official Yearbook by Cliff Butler with Ivan Ponting	£9.99
	0 233 99216 2	Manchester United Diary 1999	£4.99
	0 233 99155 7	The Official Manchester United Illustrated Encyclopedia	£25.00
	0 233 99153 0	Access All Areas by Adam Bostock and Roger Dixon	£14.99
	0 233 99417 3	The Official Manchester United Quiz Book compiled by John White	£9.99
	0 233 99498 X	For Club And Country by Gary and Phil Neville	£6.99
	0 233 99369 X	Red And Raw by Ivan Ponting	£14.99
	0 233 99616 8	The Manchester United Book Of Lists compiled by John White	£9.99
	0 233 99385 1	David Beckham: My Story by David Beckham	£8.99

All these books are available from your local bookshop or can be ordered direct from the publisher. Prices and availability are subject to change without notice.

Send order to: Manchester United Cash Sales, 76 Dean Street, London W1V 5HA.

Please send a cheque or postal order made payable to André Deutsch Ltd for the value of the book(s) and add the following for postage and packaging (remember to give your name and address)

UK: £1.00 for the first book, 50p for the second and 30p for each additional book to a maximum of £3.00

OVERSEAS including Eire: £2.00 for the first book, £1.00 for the second and 50p for each additional book to a maximum of £5.00